THE CUBAN MISSILE CRISIS

THIRTEEN DAYS ON AN ATOMIC KNIFE EDGE
OCTOBER 1962

PHIL CARRADICE

Pen & Sword
MILITARY

For my Trudy, inspirational as ever, even if you did not live to see it completed.
This one's for you, kid.

First published in Great Britain in 2017 by
PEN AND SWORD MILITARY
an imprint of
Pen and Sword Books Ltd
47 Church Street
Barnsley
South Yorkshire S70 2AS

ISBN 978 1 52670 806 9

Typeset by Aura Technology and Software Services, India
Editing and additional sourcing of photographs, Gerry van Tonder
Maps, drawings and militaria in the colour section by Colonel Dudley Wall
Printed and bound by CPI Group (UK) Ltd, Croydon, CR0 4YY

Pen & Sword Books Ltd incorporates the imprints of Pen & Sword
Archaeology, Atlas, Aviation, Battleground, Discovery, Family History, History, Maritime,
Military, Naval, Politics, Railways, Select, Social History, Transport, True Crime, Claymore Press,
Frontline Books, Leo Cooper, Praetorian Press, Remember When, Seaforth Publishing and Wharncliffe.

For a complete list of Pen and Sword titles please contact
Pen and Sword Books Limited
47 Church Street, Barnsley, South Yorkshire, S70 2AS, England
email: enquiries@pen-and-sword.co.uk
website: www.pen-and-sword.co.uk

CONTENTS

Introduction   5

1. A Personal Remembrance   7

2. Background to Crisis   12

3. Why?   29

4. Preparing Armageddon   37

5. Discovery   43

6. Addressing the Nations   53

7. Beyond Diplomacy   63

8. Black Saturday   71

9. People and Protest   81

10. An End to Crisis   101

11. Afterword   109

12. Where Are They Now?   115

    Notes   121

    Bibliography   125

    Acknowledgements   127

    About the Author   127

INTRODUCTION

On the face of it, readers could be excused for asking themselves why we need yet another book on the Cuban Missile Crisis. There are already enough of them to fill a shelf in any library. The answer is simple. Yes, this is a book about the infamous crisis of 1962 when the world came closer to extinguishing itself than ever before. But this one, I believe, is different.

To start with it was written because the publisher asked for it. That is not as crass or as glib as it sounds. The book is part of a series about the Cold War, and no account of that strange and delicately poised period would be complete without a look at the gravest moment in human history. The book fits into a sequence that, like an arch of bricks, would come crashing down if the crucial capstone happened to be missing.

There can never be too much written about a seminal event like the Cuban Missile Crisis. The only purpose behind any study of history is to learn from our mistakes and our successes. As Rudyard Kipling once said, if history was taught as a series of stories rather than a litany of dates and theories, we would all remember it much better. And not make the same mistakes again.

In keeping with that idea, this book is presented like a story, complete with characters, major and minor, each with agendas and parts to play. The story of the missile crisis is compelling and fascinating, with a plot that continually twists and turns. The exotic blends easily with the banal and the threat of destruction hangs over everything like a winter cloud.

I have never claimed to be a historian, but I do purport to be a story teller – and what better for any story teller than a tale that, in its raw form, already exists.

The three vital ingredients of all stories are here, essentials that are as important to the written word as blood and oxygen are to the human body. They are the three Ps: place, people and problem. Without them, all stories will fail, but when they combine they create a tale that is utterly, compellingly beguiling.

People – or characters – create 'reader interest' and here you have as wide a range as it is possible to find. The naïve young man who comes of age in a rites of passage experience that can hardly be bettered, the hard-bitten politician whose bullying public persona hides an inner sensitivity that will, ultimately, destroy him, and the fanatical revolutionary who will stop at nothing to guarantee the safety of his country and his own place in history. They are, to misquote many a paperback blurb, all here.

The ability to hold the reader's attention is an essential skill for any writer. I have always believed that, ever since my old history teacher, after reading one of my long and undoubtedly tedious essays on the religious settlement of Tudor England, casually tossed me a copy of Garret Mattingly's *The Defeat of the Spanish Armada* and suggested that I use it as my Bible.

'If you want to be a writer,' he declared, 'write like that.'

Mattingly's book, I discovered, was pure history, but it read like a novel. I have tried, in my own way, to follow his example ever since.

An American newspaper cartoon succinctly showing the way the world thought about the Cuban Missile Crisis – a showdown between Kennedy and Khrushchev.

There still remains the need to be accurate, to be historically correct. This book may, hopefully, read like a novel, but dates, speeches, and the all-important facts are presented as and when they occurred. There is no falsification or changing of the plot in order to heighten tension, the story does that on its own.

Interpretation? That you will find. Putting your own slant on events and people, as well as giving an opinion on policy, has always been the preserve of the historian or writer.

Lastly, it is inevitable that people involved in the crisis, either as main players or as peripheral characters, are dying. The Kennedys, Castro, Che and Khrushchev have already gone. Others will follow them in the years ahead. It will not be long before the story of the crisis is relegated from the memory of mankind to the cold, dry pages of history text books.

Nobody much below the age of 65 will have a genuine first-hand memory of the events. What they will have are stories told to them by parents, teachers, even by newspapers, which are now happy to relive it all. That is one reason why there is a chapter in the book devoted to the recollections of ordinary people who lived through the crisis, as children, as members of the armed forces, as students, and as ordinary working men and women. It is as important to record their views as it is to set down the ideas and thoughts of the big players.

All good stories need a hero and a villain, and one final way in which this book is different, is in its choice of both in the guise of one man. The tragic and ultimately doomed figure of Nikita Khrushchev strides like a modern-day King Lear across the stage where he is both hero and villain. He wears the ambiguity well, towering like a colossus over the chaos that he has created. He, not the Kennedy brothers, not Castro or Che, is the man who makes the story.

1. A PERSONAL REMEMBRANCE

In the autumn of 1962, I had just begun working for my O level examinations, studying subjects like history and Latin which, in due course, would lead to A levels and then university. But in October 1962, all that seemed a long way ahead.

I remember sitting, disinterestedly staring into space, as our history teacher stumbled into the classroom for the after-lunch session that we all called the graveyard shift. His arrival, in itself, was unusual. He normally flounced everywhere, black gown flowing like an Atlantic wave behind him. His first words, that afternoon, were not just unusual, they were terrifying.

'I don't know why I'm bothering to teach you history,' he declared, 'by this time next week we'll all be dead.'

It was a Tuesday afternoon, and for weeks now the newspapers had been droning on about growing tensions between the United States and the Soviet Union. The Americans had imposed new regulations: any ships carrying cargo to and from Cuba would no longer be allowed to dock at US ports.[1] Britain and many other European countries objected – their vessels would not be carrying arms or ammunition to Cuba. It all added to the tension.

The possibility of war between the two global superpowers was suddenly quite real and, as somebody remarked, if the next war was fought with nuclear missiles, the one

Castro and Guevara parade through Havana, after taking power, 5 March 1960.

after that would be contested with clubs and axes. Unadulterated fear was suddenly rampant, and now it seemed the Soviets had placed guided missiles on the island of Cuba.

For one reason or another, the build-up or escalation of the crisis seemed to have escaped the self-interested teenage minds of my friends and me. The nightly news programmes were just something that delayed *Bonanza*, *The Avengers* or, for the more intellectually minded, *The Sky at Night*. Therefore what was happening in the world rarely disturbed our equilibrium.

That afternoon, however, reality hit home. After his dramatic opening line, our history teacher went on to tell us about the missile crisis. With the Cold War at its height, this was the age of 'Ban the Bomb' marches, fallout shelters and Tom Lehrer singing, 'We Will All Go Together When We Go.'

So, with the phantom of communism hovering above everything like a shroud, we were prepared to listen. At the very least it meant escape for an hour or so from the boring rigours of the Agrarian and Industrial revolutions, and we willingly spent the entire lesson discussing the crisis in the Caribbean. By the end, several of the girls were in tears and I was pretty much in a similar state myself.

Those next weeks were a time of intense introspection. With typical teenage self-concern – or perhaps that should be self-deception – I thought that such feelings were limited just to me. But years later, writers are still detailing the angst they felt that bitter October:

> What was the point of continuing the human race when nuclear self-immolation seemed to be such a real and imminent possibility? That was the question that occurred to Florence as she was admitted to the delivery ward of a small country hospital in Norfolk. American air bases lay not far away, making that part of England a prime target.[2]

The Cuban Missile Crisis quickly became our sole topic of conversation. We talked about it in the playground, we debated the issues in lessons, and we loudly proclaimed our opinions on the bus during our journeys to and from school. I tried to persuade my then girlfriend that, if we were going to die, the best place was in bed – together. She quickly vetoed that idea and suggested church instead.

Of course, my father and I had discussed the missile crisis already, but I was mainly interested in playing rugby for the school and wondering what position Billy Fury's new record would reach in the charts. My father, an undisguised and unapologetic hater of all things American, was virulent in his opinions and, after a while, I usually switched off.

As the crisis deepened, however, we talked more often and in more depth. Despite myself, I actually began listening to what he had to say. Not that I always agreed with him.

My father's dislike of America stemmed from his time in Burma during the recent war. He and his comrades emerged from those steaming jungles to find that the USA, courtesy of Errol Flynn's film *Objective Burma*, was claiming to have defeated the Japanese single-handedly.

His dislike knew no bounds. I tried to tell him Flynn was actually an Australian, not American at all. And it was, after all, just a film.

'That's not the point,' he would say. 'Films like that? American propaganda, that's all they are.'

Fidel Castro meets
the writer Ernest
Hemingway who, for
a time, lived in Cuba.

And then he would be off on his pet hate.

'All those missiles on our east coast,' he'd declare, 'are pointing the wrong way. They should be aiming out over the Atlantic.'

Amazingly, during that dramatic thirteen-day period of the Cuban Missile Crisis, my father began to modify some of his opinions. Not on America and her values, but about the persona and performance of the young president, John F. Kennedy. Armageddon might be close but JFK was, he felt, the one man who might just be able to prevent the disaster.

'How come?' I asked. 'He's a Yank, isn't he?'

'Sweeping statements like that won't help anything,' said Dad, laying down his pipe and fixing me with a penetrating stare.

9

A classic portrait of John
Fitzgerald Kennedy.

'Kennedy is clever. He won't do anything stupid – which is more than can be said about his Chiefs of Staff. I met lots of American soldiers in India and, believe me, they're all the same. If they had the opportunity to nuke the Russians they would. Gung-ho, the lot of them.'

I disregarded the obvious riposte about his own sweeping statements and went back to that day's issue of the *Telegraph*.

Over the coming fortnight, we worried and we feared, plotted and planned what we would do if there was ever a missile strike on Britain. I even went so far as to draw up plans for a makeshift nuclear shelter in the garden. It would probably have lasted two seconds.

And when the crisis was finally ended, my father continued with his dislike of America and Americans – with the sole exception of JFK and, maybe, his brother Bobby.

Castro and Khrushchev embracing and pledging eternal support for each other.

'Good lads,' he would say. 'I hope they'll be around for a long while yet.'

How close the world came to wiping itself out in October 1962 remains a moot point. It would not have taken much for the USA and the USSR to resort to blows, and that would, undoubtedly, have cost millions of lives. Whether it would have spelled the end of the world is another matter.

The 'what-if?' scenario is rarely useful, but if ever there was a situation that demanded – and continues to demand – the asking of the question, it has to be the Cuban Missile Crisis. That crisis was one of the high (or low) points of the Cold War, history in the making.

When I first set foot upon Cuban soil in 2008, beyond the immediate pleasures of the Hemingway sites, and the sweeping beaches and the classic cars of Havana, the outstanding impression was one of grinding poverty. Jobs were scarce, the government stores dispensing just the bare minimum of food to enable the poor and their families to survive. The vacant stares of the pointless peasants were chilling.

The USSR had broken up and the days of Russian financial and economic aid were well gone. America remained at a distance, despite President Obama's conciliatory gestures. It was easy to look back and see the Cuba of 1962 as little more than a pawn in an international game of dubious diplomacy and highly dangerous brinkmanship.

It was a lot harder to remember that this tragic and beautiful island had once terrified us as we lay in our beds at night – conjuring Castro and Khrushchev as a demonic pair of psychotic villains, Kennedy as a knight in shining armour. The truth probably lies somewhere in between, and that is what made the Cuban Missile Crisis such a compelling subject. It still is.

2. BACKGROUND TO CRISIS

The island of Cuba lies just 93 miles off the coast of Florida. This close proximity to mainland USA has made it inevitable that American interest and involvement in Cuban affairs has, over the years, been both significant and constant.

During the nineteenth century, the American government tried, on five occasions, to buy Cuba from Spain. Then, in 1898, fate played into America's hands. There was an escalation of military activity by rebels who had always seemed to be present, stalking the hills outside Havana. The situation now was more serious than usual. The activities of rebels seeking independence from their Spanish rulers began to cause a threat, possibly more imagined than real, to American investors on the island. The US was quick to take action.

The cruiser USS *Maine* was sent to Havana to protect American interests. When she blew up and sank only three weeks after her arrival, taking over half of her crew with her to the bottom of the harbour, blame immediately fell on Spain. Nobody could prove who or what had caused the destruction of the *Maine*, but this did not stop war from breaking out.

It was a one-sided affair. The brief conflict is now best remembered for the activities of future president Teddy Roosevelt and his Roughriders on San Juan Hill, before the war stuttered to an inevitable American victory. With peace, came the creation of an independent Cuba, albeit one under heavy US protection and with a considerable American garrison stationed on the island.

The USS *Maine* enters Havana harbour. One of the most powerful ships in the US Navy, she would soon be resting on the harbour bed.

The 1899 Platt Amendment provided the basis for American influence. Among other terms, it did actually look to the future, albeit a distant one. In particular, it agreed to American forces leaving Cuba and a transfer of sovereignty to the Cubans themselves, but only when the Cuban government was prepared to adhere to eight specific conditions.

These included the Cubans denying foreign powers use of the island for military purposes and, importantly, giving the USA the right to intervene in Cuban affairs in order to defend her independence. One clause or condition that was almost immediately taken up, was the leasing of land on Cuba to the US for use as a naval station, leading to a lease in perpetuity for the Guantanamo Bay naval base, a tiny piece of America on Cuban soil.

Cuba may have been technically independent, but throughout the first half of the twentieth century, American influence on the island was vast. Economic and industrial influence provided the corner stone of American strength. Between 1913 and 1928, US investments in Cuba increased by an amazing 536 per cent. America was now the chief market for Cuban exports, sugar in particular, and at the same time the US had become the primary source of imports into the island.[1]

By the early 1930s, the US owned nearly 80 per cent of all Cuba's sugar production and 90 per cent of the copper-mining industry. In addition, American investors and businessmen held major shares in all the railways, oil refineries, banks and electrical firms.[2]

During the 1920s, the island was invariably in a state of chaos. To outside observers, there seemed to be an almost continual series of revolutions, accompanied by the overthrow of one leader after the other. When Franklin Delano 'FDR' Roosevelt became president of the US in 1933, Cuban leaders and the Americans felt that the Platt Amendment was increasingly being used to pull the US into Cuban affairs, something that FDR did not want and which, America, still struggling its way out of the Depression, could not afford.

In 1934 came Fulgencio Batista's successful Sergeants' Revolt, so-called because future dictator Batista was

LABOURERS IN CANE FIELD

Workers in a cane field. The production of sugar cane was crucial to the Cuban economy in the early twentieth century, even though the US took most of the profits.

An early advertising postcard showing the delights of Cuba – for those who could afford it.

then a sergeant in the Cuban army. Batista did not take power at this time, but set up a puppet regime, clearly backed by him and with a suitable pro-American bias. Accepting this, the US agreed to the abrogation of the Platt Amendment. However, even after 1934, American investors retained their hold on the island's industries, courtesy of investments in projects such as tourist hotels and gambling, much of it being 'mob' related.

It meant that throughout the 1930s and 1940s, Cuba was an island of decadence and bonhomie – as long as you were rich. For those with money, it was a land of luxury hotels, gambling, dancing and deep-sea fishing. But for the poor, it was a daily effort to survive, a hand-to-mouth existence where disease and squalor were the best people could hope for.

Despite being the largest of the Caribbean nations, compared to the USA Cuba was a small and relatively insignificant territory. However, by the early 1960s the island had assumed an importance that was far beyond its size and strength. Much of this was due to its new president, Fidel Castro.

Fidel Alejandro Castro Ruz came from a privileged family, but he was badly behaved at school and unable to tolerate criticism or attempts at control. A Jesuit-run boarding school was felt to be the answer, but his bad behaviour continued.

He somehow stumbled through his school years and eventually enrolled at university in Havana to study law.

He was a revolutionary from his days at university, and in 1953, his failed attempt to storm the Moncada Barracks at Santiago led to prison and exile in Mexico. Undaunted, he

In the 1930s and 1940s, Cuba was a tourist paradise, offering good food, good wine and everything money could buy.

Young Fidel Castro in the days before he grew his distinctive beard. Known as *Los Barbudos* (the bearded ones), Castro's rebels were proud of their facial hair – the longer your beard, the longer you had served the revolution.

continued to plot against the dictator Batista, who had now seized power himself and was milking the island for every penny he could find.

Castro eventually returned to Cuba, along with the revolutionary Che Guevara and a small party of Cuban freedom fighters. They disembarked from the yacht *Granma*, landing in a mangrove swamp. Those who survived the murderous gunfire from Batista's soldiers were forced to walk and crawl inland. The two Castro brothers, Fidel and Raúl, and Che Guevara and fifteen others were all that survived from an original group of nearly 100 men – hardly an auspicious beginning. They had been lucky to reach Cuba. The yacht was supposed to have a capacity of no more than twenty-five. Che later said that this wasn't a landing, more of a shipwreck! Whatever it was, Castro was back.

In December 1959, after two years of guerrilla activity from their base in the Sierra Maestra mountains, Castro and his 26 July Movement (the date of Castro's unsuccessful attack on the Moncada Barracks) succeeded in overthrowing the corrupt government of the hated and pro-American dictator, Fulgencio Batista.

Above: The tiny yacht *Granma* on which Castro and his supporters, after a period of exile in Mexico, returned to Cuba. Incredibly, this boat held the hundred or so revolutionaries who landed on Cuba.

Right: The dictator Fulgencio Batista in formal uniform.

Above left: Che Guevara and Fidel Castro celebrate the success of their revolution.

Above right: Guevara, revolutionary hero of the 1960s, is shown here on a publicity postcard.

When he came to power, and despite the involvement and support of outright Marxists like Che Guevara, Castro was certainly not a communist. He was simply a revolutionary, albeit one with leftist and decidedly anti-American leanings.

Over the next few years, Castro ruthlessly set about establishing a secure power base, creating a regime founded on his own idiosyncratic brand of Marxist/Leninist thinking. Show-trials and executions of Batista's officials were just the start. Despite many of his early reforms – like enhancing the status of women – the Cuban people were split, many welcoming his regime, others bitterly opposing it.

Castro always had much in common, ideologically at least, with communist superpowers like Russia. Consequently, in the summer of 1960 he announced to the world that, in future, his regime would be under the support of – and provided with arms by – the Soviet Union.

It was the beginning of a tense period of international politics. Cuba under Batista had, for twenty years, been on favourable terms with America, but now the administration of President Eisenhower was faced by an openly unhelpful regime just a few miles off their coast. Within a year, private land ownership in Cuba was abolished and over $850 million worth of US property and businesses on the island was nationalized. In retaliation, President Eisenhower promptly embargoed Cuba's vital sugar market in the US.

Potentially devastating as this was, all the embargo achieved was to push Castro further into the arms of Soviet Russia. Soviet Premier Nikita Khrushchev agreed that the USSR

Right: President Eisenhower found himself on the wrong end of Castro's successful revolution on Cuba.

Below: Eisenhower, Khrushchev and their wives – the smiles are false, the dresses are genuine.

would buy all the sugar that the US no longer wanted while, at the same time, arms shipments to the island would be stepped up.[3]

Since the end of the Second World War, American governments had been increasingly paranoid about the worldwide growth of communism. Now, the open alliance between a Latin American country – a Latin American country that was, almost literally, in America's back yard – and the USSR was deeply troubling.

The alliance of Castro and Khrushchev was in direct contravention to the Monroe Doctrine. This long-standing American policy had been designed in 1823, declaring that US involvement in European affairs would be limited. At the same time, European powers should have little or no interaction with independent states or countries in the western part of the globe. That was to be the domain of the USA.[4]

By March 1960, Dwight Eisenhower, in the last stages of his presidency, was reluctant to see his country branded an outright aggressor towards smaller nations. Yet safety issues and international diplomacy demanded that he do something about the Cuban problem.

Instead of the US-led invasion that his advisors were urging, Eisenhower agreed to a proposal from the Central Intelligence Agency (CIA) to fund and equip a group of Cuban exiles who would land on the island, overthrow Castro and establish an 'acceptable' regime. No American troops would take part in the invasion, although the US, through the CIA, would be prepared to provide air and naval support.

The badge and emblem of Brigade 2506, the para-military unit of Cuban exiles raised in the USA to invade Cuba.

A small group of just twenty-eight Cuban exiles was recruited to form what was supposedly a crack guerrilla unit known as Brigade 2506. Within a few months, the size of the unit had increased to nearly 1,500. They were trained at various bases in Panama, where they were intended to become experts at covert operations and jungle warfare.

Over $13 million was allocated to fund the assault on Cuba, but delays meant that Eisenhower was out of office long before the paramilitary force was ready. It fell to the new president, John F. Kennedy to decide whether or not the invasion should take place. It was something of a poisoned chalice, but he approved the attack in the spring of 1961. On 17 April the assault was launched.

The Bay of Pigs invasion – named after the area where the main assault was to take place – turned out to be a disaster. Brigade 2506 had been infiltrated by Castro's spies and, consequently, the unit's movements and plans were known in Havana almost before they set out.

Badly organized, badly led and badly informed, the men of Brigade 2506 found themselves up against the full weight of the Cuban army, led by Castro himself. They were out-manoeuvred and out-fought, and with world opinion immediately

Premier Khrushchev and President Kennedy chat happily together – for the moment.

condemning the obvious American involvement, Kennedy refused to sanction vital air and naval support. After just three days, the Cuban exiles surrendered. David had beaten Goliath!

Apart from having to negotiate and pay for the release of the surviving members of Brigade 2506, American prestige plummeted. More important was Kennedy's standing in the eyes of the USSR.

To Khrushchev, it seemed that the new president was both weak and indecisive in moments of crisis. Kennedy's lack of experience left the young man unsuited, the Russian premier believed, for the deadly game of brinkmanship that dominated the Cold War period. As Kennedy himself knew, and later declared, Khrushchev's opinion of him was indeed unflattering: 'I'm inexperienced. He [Khrushchev] probably thinks I'm stupid. Maybe most important, he thinks that I have no guts.'[5]

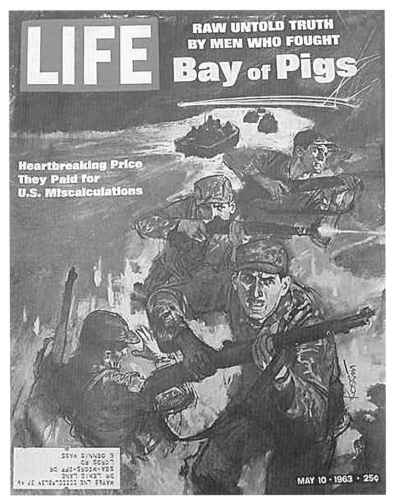

The Bay of Pigs invasion was a total disaster. *Life* magazine's May 10th edition led with this rather stylized cover.

When the two leaders met at a summit conference in Vienna in June 1961, Khrushchev treated his American counterpart with disdain. He hectored and brow-beat Kennedy, lecturing him on the iniquities of capitalism. He threatened that he would soon march into West Berlin and showed a very flippant attitude towards the menace of nuclear war. Observers, like British Prime Minister Harold MacMillan and Kennedy's own Vice-President Lyndon B. Johnson, were dismayed at the president's inability to hold his own with Khrushchev.

The Russian opinion of Kennedy was confirmed when the Berlin Wall was created in August 1961. The American response was, at best, restrained and arguably, even non-existent. The USA, President Kennedy declared, would not oppose building the barrier.

The presence of American, British and French forces in Berlin – deep inside East Germany – had long been a source of irritation to the Soviets. Building the wall was both a statement and a means of stemming the tide of fleeing Germans desperate for the greater freedoms of the West.

Given the preponderance of Soviet tanks and artillery in and around Berlin, US military action was never a realistic option. Even so, the Soviet threat to the city and its population did not go away. It was something that would figure largely in the thinking of Kennedy and his advisors during the Cuban crisis.

After failure at the Bay of Pigs, American opposition to Castro's regime slipped into a curious, almost comical world of unreality. As part of what was known as Operation

The city of Berlin, divided into occupied zones and central to the events of the Cuban Missile Crisis.

Mongoose, CIA agents were infiltrated into Cuba to begin a campaign of sabotage. There was even a wild suggestion that American forces should attack targets in the USA and then blame the carnage on Cuba. Kennedy promptly vetoed that suggestion.

That was not the only dangerous idea to come out of this period. One proposal called for US submarines to approach Cuba at night, surface, and then fire star shells over the island. The gigantic firework display would convince the superstitious and highly religious Cubans that they were witnessing the Second Coming of Christ.

The Mafia were sounded out about the possibility of assassinating Castro but, more ludicrous yet, was the scheme to poison the trademark cigars of the Cuban leader so that he lost his beard, making him a laughing stock with his people. In all, Castro survived over 300 CIA planned attempts on his life – which says more about the inefficiency of the CIA than it does about Castro's luck.

On 2 December 1961, Castro's bombshell announcement that his regime would henceforth follow a rigid Marxist/Leninist programme caused incredulity in the USA.

It was an announcement that was received with mixed feelings in Cuba. Castro's sister Juanita, later forced into exile by her opposition to his regime, was particularly scathing:

> As I listened, I thought that surely he must be a superb actor. He had fooled not only so many of his friends but his family as well. In his speech, he said he had been a communist practically all his life. Yet how could Fidel, who had been given the best of everything, be a Communist? This was the riddle which paralyzed me and so many other Cubans.[6]

An American U-2 spy plane sits on the tarmac.

Castro's sister Juanita Castro, scathing of her brother's so-called communist sentiments.

Castro's announcement was a public one, on a TV chat show, and in the wake of the Bay of Pigs fiasco, was not something that Kennedy's Joint Chiefs of Staff could ignore. Increasingly belligerent and bellicose, the Chiefs of Staff – air force General Curtis LeMay in particular – were soon lobbying Kennedy for a pre-emptive strike on Cuba, followed by a full-scale invasion.

To the Chiefs of Staff, the prospect of a communist regime in the western hemisphere was too awful to contemplate, a regime that might soon start to spread its influence across other Latin American nations. What was conveniently ignored was the fact that, at that time, Castro had little interest in spreading communism to anyone. What concerned him was the security of his island and his own position as head of state.

Partly in response to the pressure from his military advisors, however, in February 1962 Kennedy instigated a full embargo against Cuba. Contact between America, where thousands of Cubans had taken refuge from the Castro regime, and the island immediately ceased.

Soviet Premier Nikita Khrushchev was nothing if not a showman. With tension already taut as a bow string, he now proceeded to lay the ground for what he hoped would be a crushing blow to American status and power. Choosing his moment with

Nikita Khrushchev portrayed
here on a Russian stamp.

infinite care, in May 1962 he made the decision to place guided missiles on Cuba. It was, to put it mildly, a terribly risky strategy, as Fidel Castro later noted: 'We preferred the risks of great tension ... to the risks of the impotence of having to wait for a United States invasion of Cuba.'[7]

Despite those words, Castro was at first reluctant to allow the missiles to be placed in Cuba. He did not wish to be seen merely as a Soviet puppet. That summer, both Raúl Castro and Che Guevara led delegations to Moscow, where for several weeks there was much discussion with Khrushchev and his advisors.

Eventually, Castro changed his mind about the missiles. Placement of nuclear weapons would, he began to believe, infuriate the Americans, while also providing the island with a high degree of safety and security.

If Castro's announcement about his political stance had caused anxiety in US government circles, the prospect of a well-armed Cuba provoked utter consternation. Kennedy had made the missile gap and the supposed Soviet lead in the nuclear arms race one of the key issues of his 1960 campaign for the presidency. In fact, the USSR lay a long way behind the Americans and, in 1961, possessed only a handful of intercontinental ballistic missiles, compared to America's 170.[8]

No US administration could afford to ignore the prospect of hostile forces located within striking distance of America's eastern seaboard. At this stage, there was no mention of what Kennedy termed offensive nuclear missiles, but the fear and tension were real enough. Kennedy knew that public opinion was fickle. If his administration did not take a strong line, then not only would the looming mid-term elections be disastrous, but his Republican opponent in the 1964 presidential election would be bound to make capital out of it.

Being seen as a weak and indecisive president would destroy Kennedy's hopes of a second term. His opponent and probable successor would most certainly campaign on the issue, the prospect of Russian missiles just 90 miles away from Key West offering a very handy stick with which to beat the present incumbent of the White House.

The Castro brothers, Fidel and Raúl, visiting Cuban troops in the field.

As yet there was no evidence that the USSR was doing anything more than posturing, an act at which Khrushchev was particularly adept. He had, after all, recently boasted to the whole world about the number of missiles the USSR was building – producing them 'like sausages', he famously declared, when, as was later proved, his assertions were nothing more than empty rhetoric.

For his part, Khrushchev remained sanguine about the American response to greater Soviet aid for Cuba. In a conversation with American Interior Secretary Stewart Udall on 6 September 1961, he commented simply that:

> A lot of people are making a big fuss because we are giving aid to Cuba. But you are giving aid to Japan. Just recently I was reading that you have placed atomic warheads on Japanese territory and surely this is not something the Japanese need. So, when Castro comes to us for aid, we give him what he needs for defence.[9]

No mention was made of offensive nuclear weapons, but it was clear to everyone, even at this early stage of the crisis, that the nuclear option would be the next logical step. However, when in May 1962 Khrushchev and Castro did finally agree to the placing of nuclear missiles in Cuba, it was a decision that they both felt needed to be kept secret.

The original aim was to clandestinely build the missile sites, bring in the weapons, then say nothing until after the 1964 US presidential elections. Then, in a dramatic and theatrical gesture, Khrushchev would reveal their presence at the United Nations General Assembly. It would, Khrushchev believed, stop the Americans in their tracks and help him obtain concessions over Berlin.

The plan was a major gamble and, considering the sophisticated nature of US surveillance of Cuba, one that was never likely to succeed.[10]

As early as 12 September, US reconnaissance reported a twelve-strong truck convoy operating to the south-west of the Cuban capital, Havana. The trucks were apparently carrying long cylindrical objects, like giant cigar tubes, perhaps 65–70ft in length, objects that could very easily have been missiles. High-altitude reconnaissance flights by Lockheed U-2 aircraft had to be reinstated.[11]

The surveillance aircraft had been stood down on 30 August when an air force U2 mistakenly flew over Sakhalin Island, a Soviet territory in the Far East. The pause in flights was in order to minimize Russian protests and prevent a major diplomatic incident. Following the destruction of a Republic of China (Taiwan) U-2 on 8 September, shot down over China by a SAM missile, there was fear that the Cubans or the Soviets might have the same success above Cuba.

Consequently, Secretary of State Dean Rusk and National Security Advisor McGeorge Bundy stopped the U-2 flights, thus implementing a five-week 'photo gap' when no high-level reconnaissance of Cuba took place. Attempts to use a Corona Photo Reconnaissance Satellite to gain information were unsuccessful due to bad weather, and the 'gap' was only closed when Kennedy ordered the U-2 coverage to begin again.

Importantly, Kennedy did not have the power to declare war, but his was the controlling voice, albeit with guidance from his Joint Chiefs of Staff, when it came to the deployment of weapons. Only Congress had the right to declare war on other nations.

What the arrangement had in its favour was that it created a system of checks and balances to prevent hasty actions and ill-timed mistakes. But it was also a cumbersome process, which demanded combined decision-making, particularly between politicians and the military – not easy to achieve in a situation like the Cuban Missile Crisis where responses had to be quick as well as fully thought through.[12]

This was the situation in September 1963. Expectations were high, anxiety even higher. Cold War tensions seemed to have settled like a mist over Washington and Moscow, and nobody could say where or when that tension would break out into open hostility.

It is hard not to invoke the oft-used metaphor of the Doomsday Clock, which has now become something of a cliché. Nevertheless, it is an appropriate image to catch the anxiety of those early days of the Cuban Missile Crisis. The hands of that imaginary but terrifying clock had, most certainly, edged closer towards the witching hour of midnight. They were, in the days and weeks ahead, to move even closer still.

US Secretary of State Dean Rusk.

3. WHY?

By the first days of September 1962, the drama was ready to begin, the stage set and the main participants in place, waiting for their cues. Of the main players, it would be difficult to imagine two more diametrically opposite individuals than the leaders of the USA and the USSR.

John Fitzgerald Kennedy was the scion of a wealthy New England family, whose ancestors had left Ireland for a new life in the USA. His father, Joseph, was a businessman and politician who had been American ambassador to Britain during the war years. A driven, often brutal individual, who viewed Britain with an almost pathological dislike, Joe Kennedy reared his family to take up positions of influence and power.

At school, John F. Kennedy found himself in the shadow of his elder brother, Joseph Jr, who was not only a fine scholar, but also an athlete of note. John, or Jack as he was known within the family, reacted by becoming something of a rebel, much given to practical jokes and high jinks.

He was beset by poor health during his childhood and adolescence. He was then severely injured during the Second World War when his PT boat was cut in half during operations in the Pacific. Those wartime injuries were to stay with him for the rest of his life, necessitating the wearing of a back brace to ease the constant pain in his spine.

Almost all his adulthood – certainly for his time in the White House – Kennedy had serious health problems, and was forced to take medicines and potions to cope with his ailments. In addition to his war wound, these included Addison's disease and nagging stomach, colon and prostate problems. He suffered from urinary infections and from an abscess, which may or may not have been related to a venereal problem he had picked up as an adolescent. He also suffered from chronic lower-back pain stemming from excessive steroid therapy when he was a young man. With all the medication he was taking, Kennedy was a walking pharmacist's shop.

Castro at the UN General Assembly, 1960.
(Photo Warren K. Leffler)

The top job, the presidency, had been reserved for the eldest Kennedy boy. Unfortunately, Joseph Kennedy Jr, a navy pilot, was killed while on a bombing mission in August 1944. Jack was promptly elevated to take his place. Carefree days were over as he bowed to his father's imposing will and began his political career, as a senator and congressman. In 1960, he became the first Catholic president of the USA – and the youngest incumbent of the post.

Physically attractive, Kennedy was also socially adept. Despite his 'film-star' marriage to the elegant and beautiful Jacqueline Bouvier – which, in the eyes of many Americans, symbolized a new beginning, a new Camelot – he was always something of a womanizer. A probable affair with Marilyn Monroe was just the tip of the iceberg.

Nikita Khrushchev was the complete opposite. Poorly educated, he was born into a peasant family in the year 1894 in the tiny village of Kalinovka, close to the Russian border with Ukraine. His early days were hard. There was little money for such fripperies as fine food and formal education.

After the inevitable period of work on the family smallholding, Khrushchev was employed, at the age of 15, as a metalworker. He was excused military service in the

The Kennedy brothers, John and Bobby, with J. Edgar Hoover, director of the FBI. (Courtesy Albie Rowe)

First World War because of the importance of his job, but during the Russian Civil War he became a political commissar. From that relatively humble beginning, he began a slow rise through the ranks of the Soviet regime.

Khrushchev was a latecomer to the communist party, only joining in 1918. Despite this, in 1931 he became district secretary of the party in Moscow, followed in 1938 by the appointment as first secretary in the Ukraine. In 1939, he joined the Politburo, the 'inner cabinet' of the party.[1]

Khrushchev was fortunate to survive the purges of the 1930s. Many of his comrades did not. He was, at that stage, an unashamed supporter of Stalin – a major factor in his survival – and of the whole concept of purging the regime. This was to change after Stalin's death and his own rise to the top. He was a political opportunist, but one with a rare gift for survival in a world steeped in treachery and double-dealing.

During the Second World War, Khrushchev was again a political commissar, a dangerous position, which would have meant instant execution if he had ever been captured by the Germans. He was immensely proud of being present during the siege of Stalingrad. It was, in the eyes of many Russians, a badge of extraordinary courage.

Short, rotund, looking far more like a Russian peasant than a politician, Khrushchev adopted the pose of a loud-mouthed bully. Taking off his shoe to bang it on the table at the United Nations typified his public persona, but this bully-like appearance and manner belied an astute brain and a degree of compassion that most western governments would never have recognized. He confessed, in private, to actually feeling sorry for Kennedy during their encounter at Vienna in 1961.

He also had an incisive sense of humour, albeit one laced with the coarse or earthy language you might expect from a man with his background. Two comments about the USA and the missile crisis are typical of the man: 'I am going to put a hedgehog down the pants of the Americans' and 'Cuba – the testicles of the Americans. If I want them to squirm a little, I just squeeze gently.'

Khrushchev became chairman of the Council of Ministers, or premier, in 1958, making him the Soviet leader throughout JFK's time in the White House. Under Stalin, the ideals of the Russian Revolution had given way to a dystopian and draconian dictatorship, where

Khrushchev at a meeting of the United Nations in New York – the face and pose he chose to present to the world.

high officials had their own driving lanes on the motorways and everyone feared the KGB's midnight knock on the door.

Possibly half a million so-called 'enemies of the people' were exiled to Siberia or executed on Khrushchev's orders during Stalin's reign of terror, but after the dictator's death, the USSR underwent a process of gradual de-Stalinization, a loosening of the iron fist that had marked Stalin's period in power. Many, if not most, of the reforms were down to one man – Nikita Khrushchev, who publicly denounced his former chief. Democratic the USSR was certainly not, but it was, at least, a start.

In hindsight, it is difficult to see what Khrushchev hoped to achieve by placing nuclear missiles on Cuba. He must have known that the USA would react, but he firmly believed that Kennedy was weak. While the Americans would protest, maybe even threaten, they would stop short of any warlike action. As he told his son Sergei, President Kennedy would make a fuss, then make even more of a fuss, and finally agree to everything.[2]

Khrushchev's appraisal of Kennedy was, in fact, quite wrong, but he was operating only on the known facts and on the young president's performance so far. That performance had certainly not been good.

It is possible that Kennedy's poor showing at the Vienna Conference in 1961 was due less to political naïveté than to the cocktail of drugs he was taking. The president's various ailments and the medication he was imbibing throughout his time in the White House, were kept hidden from the American public. It was not a deliberate device to fool Khrushchev, but keeping quiet about Kennedy's illnesses certainly misled the Kremlin at a vital and dangerous time.

Neither the Bay of Pigs fiasco nor the conference at Vienna filled the Russians with trepidation. Even so, Khrushchev, along with Castro and other members of the Soviet

Havana, la Habana. (Photo Yeoztudioz)

hierarchy, were convinced that an American invasion of Cuba was imminent. This not only affected their thinking at this time but also their actions.

Again, Khrushchev got it wrong. A US attack on Castro's island was certainly not on the American agenda, despite continued 'raids' by Cuban exiles. National Security Advisor McGeorge Bundy later made it clear. An American attack, he stated, 'would mean open war against Cuba which, in the US judgement, is not advisable in the present international situation.'[3]

Despite possessing only 20 intercontinental ballistic missiles (ICBMs), which would be capable of hitting US targets from their bases in Russia, what the USSR did have in some quantity was around 700 medium- and intermediate-range missiles (MRBMs and IRBMs). Most of these were located in Eastern Europe.

In 1962, the Kremlin's short-term answer to the problem was to ignore, as far as possible, the intercontinental ballistic missile gap, and concentrate on placing medium- and intermediate-range missiles in countries where they could hit designated targets in America. Cuba quickly became an important part of this strategy.

After discussion with his military chiefs, Khrushchev decided to build several missile sites on the Caribbean island, missile sites that would deploy 24 medium-range R12 missiles, each with a range of just over 1,000 miles. Sixteen R14 missiles, with a range of 2,100 miles, would also be sent to Cuba. It meant that not just the eastern states lay in their range, but so too were a number of other regions and major cities. In the words of Bobby Kennedy, 'The estimate was that within a few minutes of their being fired, eighty million Americans would be dead.'[4]

In addition to the missiles, 44,000 Russian support workers and 1,300 civilian construction workers would be posted to the island. A plan to build a nuclear submarine base on Cuba, however, was soon shelved as being too provocative. Instead of nuclear submarines, Khrushchev sent four diesel-electric Foxtrot-class submarines to the area: 'The Foxtrots were larger, updated versions of the German U Boats that had harassed Allied shipping in World War Two. The difference was that they each carried a small, nuclear tipped torpedo, in addition to twenty-one conventional torpedoes.'[5]

Khrushchev had never intended the missiles on the island to be fired. He had no wish to start a war which, ultimately, nobody could win. The missiles were there simply to frighten the Americans – the great 'bluffer' in action once again – and to 'give them a taste of their own medicine'.

In April 1962, a month before Khrushchev and Castro agreed to placing nuclear weapons on Cuba, the US had installed fifteen intermediate-range missiles in Turkey. These Jupiter rockets were virtually obsolete, but they were a reaffirmation of American superiority in the nuclear stakes. Perhaps more importantly, along with missiles in West Germany, Italy and Japan, the weapons completed a virtual encircling of the USSR.

Russian missiles on Cuba would show the Americans how it felt to be threatened. This nuclear brinkmanship was a dangerous game to play, but Khrushchev had been reared on the revolutionary cut and thrust of politics in Bolshevik Russia. To him, international

US Jupiter missiles installed in Turkey.

diplomacy would always be a process of bluff and counter-bluff. It was just a case of who could hold their nerve the longest.

In many ways, at this early stage of the crisis, Khrushchev held by far the strongest hand. Under international law, the USSR had every right to send nuclear missiles to Cuba, just as Castro and his regime had every right to receive them. The negotiations and the transaction were nothing to do with the USA – at least in theory.[6] The way that America perceived the threat, however, was a different matter altogether.

Yet another reason for the placement of missiles on Cuba, unconnected as it might at first seem, was the city of Berlin. Occupied since the war by the four main Allied powers – America, Britain, Russia and France – the previous capital city of Germany was situated well inside the eastern part of the now divided country.

The four-country occupation of Berlin would not have been a problem for the Soviet Union, except for the city's location. In the minds of the Soviet planners and strategists, it was a threat to the security of their puppet state of East Germany and, by default, of the USSR as well.

With Berlin occupying a central role in the Cold War politics of the time, Khrushchev was convinced that he could trade off the Cuban missiles for the American presence in West Berlin. It was a simple matter of barter – we will remove the Cuban missiles if you pull out of West Berlin.

Kennedy later agreed that it was a good tactic, but it was also dangerous. Everything really depended on the metal of the new, young American president and his desire to maintain America's moral standing.[7]

Khrushchev's need to improve Russian political influence in the world, while retaining his own power within the USSR, were significant factors. His inability to broker a settlement regarding Berlin was something that had hurt his position greatly, as was the country's failure to hit the food-production targets that he had recently set. The targets might have been unrealistic, but failing to reach them was, in the eyes of the ruling Soviet elite, a grave error.[8]

There was also the little matter of China. When the Chinese Communist Party under Mao Zedong came to power in 1949, the change of Chinese leadership had been greatly welcomed in Moscow. On the other hand, it was something that was feared in the West. The thought of an enormous Marxist power block ranging from Europe to the shores of the Pacific had been almost too terrifying to contemplate.

In fact, the two communist powers had little in common. Traditional Marxist theory declared that a true proletarian revolution could only occur in an industrial society. China, though developing rapidly, was still largely rural, with its economy based on agriculture. Therefore, the Soviets believed, it could not be regarded as a fully rounded communist country. Annoyed at this attitude, the Chinese retaliated by claiming that Russia had betrayed world revolution by its anxiety to form alliances with the capitalist countries of the West.[9]

Relations between China and the USSR became increasingly brittle. There were disputes over territory, and incidents between Russian and Chinese troops along their mutual border had not made things any easier.

Mao Zedong and Khrushchev looking relaxed and happy. The two men actually disliked each other intensely.

By 1962, both the USSR and China were claiming leadership of world communism. Success in Cuba, Khrushchev believed, and a humbling of the United States would only reinforce the claims of the Soviet Union to that honour.

It was not long before theories became practicalities. Throughout the early months of 1962, there was 'a relentless build-up of Eastern Bloc armaments' on Cuba.[10] Most of these weapons were defensive in nature – anti-aircraft missiles – but the increase in military supplies brought huge anxiety to the US government and great joy to Castro and his supporters.

Hit-and-run raids by Cuban exiles based in America continued. Hardly as dramatic as the Bay of Pigs fiasco, these raids were worrying for Castro. CIA reports were clear that a number of incidents, although perhaps small in scale, were significant in their effect: 'These incidents have given Havana the jitters. The army, as well as the navy, has been alerted. One of our naval aircraft on a routine mission, was fired on yesterday afternoon by Cuban patrol vessels at a point twelve miles off the Cuban coast.'[11]

Fidel Castro, perceptive and cunning at the same time, was well aware of the personalities of the men he was working with and against, Khrushchev in particular.

The two men had first met on 20 September 1960 in New York for a meeting of the United Nations General Assembly. They had embraced after a chance encounter on a street in Harlem – a difficult gesture for a man of 6ft 4in and another just 5ft 3in – and immediately hit it off.

Both Castro and Khrushchev were anti-American revolutionaries, something Castro never forgot, often reminding the more recalcitrant members of the Kremlin that he and they came from similar political backgrounds. The success of Castro's revolution was the stuff of romance, just as the Bolshevik Revolution of 1917 occupied a precious place in the hearts and minds of the old left wing activists in the Kremlin:

'The Cubans were well aware of the effect they were having on the Soviets and used it to their advantage. "Nikita loved Cuba very much," Castro would recall. "He had a weakness for Cuba, you might say."'[12]

Khrushchev was not naïve. He would not have allowed his affection for Cuba and for Castro – even though he claimed to love the revolutionary leader 'like a son' – to influence his decisions. His reasons for placing missiles on the island might have led him in the wrong direction, just as his assessment of Kennedy was equally wrong, but they were not driven by emotion.

Where his obvious affection for Castro did come into play was at the subliminal level. In a way, it was reminiscent of Harold swearing an oath to make William of Normandy King of England in 1066. Logically, such an occurrence had little or no effect on the Battle of Hastings – or did it? Was the fear of breaking an oath made before God something that played on Harold's mind throughout that tempestuous day?

It might well have been the same with Khrushchev, leaving us to ask whether or not his strong emotions tilted the balance and made him act in the way that he did. It is, at least, an intriguing hypothesis.

4. PREPARING ARMAGEDDON

In early July 1962, Premier Khrushchev and Defence Secretary Rodion Malinovsky approved the Soviet plans to turn Cuba into what Malinovsky called 'an impregnable fortress'.[1] Gathering together weapons and equipment, while trying to remain 'under the radar', took far longer than was planned. The first ship, the merchant vessel *Omsk*, left Odessa on 25 August with its cargo of eight R12 missiles. Operation Anadyr was under way.

Secrecy was crucial. Nobody knew the destination of this first ship, neither the watching Americans, nor the Soviet soldiers and sailors themselves. For all anybody knew, the freighter *Omsk* could have been headed into the blackness of oblivion.

Felt winter clothing, fur hats and ski boots had been loaded onto the ship in a rather idiosyncratic attempt to fool any watching spies into believing that the expedition was bound for arctic climates. Only when the *Omsk* had passed Gibraltar and was well out into the Atlantic was the sealed packet of orders opened. It was immediately clear that warm winter clothing would not be needed. Their destination was Cuba.

It was an uncomfortable journey. Pride of place on the ship went to the eight R12 missiles, which had to be kept below deck in the holds, leaving nearly 300 men of the missile battery to crowd into cramped spaces that normally held deck cargo. Hatches were bolted shut. The combination of heat from the relentless sun, lack of fresh air, motion of the ship and sweating bodies soon made sea sickness endemic.

The Americans were suspicious, and as the *Omsk* neared Cuban waters, their surveillance intensified. Reconnaissance aircraft and patrol boats investigated and photographed the freighter, but the missiles were well hidden down below. Short of stopping and boarding the ship, something that would be perilously close to an act of war, there was little more that could be done.

Intercepted Russian messages eventually convinced the American watchers that the *Omsk* was carrying nothing more dangerous than gas oil, and surveillance was relaxed. In the absence of hard photographic evidence, it is possible that the Americans were

ПОЧТА СССР 1973

МАРШАЛ СОВЕТСКОГО СОЮЗА
Р. Я. МАЛИНОВСКИЙ
1898-1967

Soviet Defence Secretary Rodion Malinovsky, shown here on a Russian stamp.

fooling themselves, not wishing to believe that the Soviets would be reckless enough to bring offensive nuclear missiles into Cuba.

Whatever the Americans thought, the *Omsk* rounded Cuba and sailed, untroubled, past the US base at Guantanamo Bay. On 8 September, she docked at Casilda, a small port on Cuba's south coast, well away from the logical destination of Havana. Unloading slowly, and then only at night, it took three days of gruelling manual effort before the first consignment of Soviet missiles was ashore.

Transporting the missiles to their base close to the town of Sagua la Grande in the north took another three nights, with the transports hidden and the drivers catching up on sleep during daylight hours. A few miles outside Sagua la Grande were two pre-prepared sites with four rocket launchers in each, all of them well camouflaged.

The Soviet Union did not deny that they were sending weapons to Cuba. They had been openly doing that since Castro and Khrushchev first came to an agreement back in 1960. Now, however, they repeatedly denied that the weapons they were sending were offensive – surface-to-surface guided missiles that could be launched against the USA – and insisted that what they were supplying was purely defensive in nature: anti-aircraft guns and missiles for use only against aerial targets. They were, the Soviet ambassador told Adlai Stevenson at the United Nations on 7 September, there to support the Cubans in the event of an American attack.

By the middle of October, the Soviet regime was still maintaining the deception. On the 17th, the day after the White House learned about the presence of what were termed

A Soviet freighter approaching Cuba, with an American P-2 Neptune reconnaissance aircraft flying low overhead.

offensive missiles on Cuba, Khrushchev sent a personal message to President Kennedy stating that the Soviet missiles were 'purely defensive'. If it had not been so serious, the lie might have made Kennedy laugh.

While still not wanting to believe the USSR was sending weapons of mass destruction to Cuba, in September Congress approved US Joint Resolution 230, resolving to prevent any foreign interventions – for 'foreign', read Soviet – on the island. The president was authorized to take any steps necessary to deal with external forces that threatened the security of the nation. Constitutionally, Kennedy now had a free hand, while Castro became more convinced than ever that an American invasion of Cuba was imminent.

Soviet missile specialists had been on the island since July, operating under the guise of agricultural and irrigation specialists and, in the wake of the *Omsk*, eighty-five Eastern Bloc cargo ships left ports on the Black Sea. The second shipload of R12 missiles arrived in Cuba on 16 September, and by the middle of October, there were nearly 40,000 Soviet troops stationed on the island. The CIA estimated the number at no more than 8,000, but the intelligence agency was out by many thousands in its calculations – a potentially disastrous error.

Three missile regiments manned and operated the R12 rockets, with two more preparing for the coming of the R14s – still on board ship somewhere out in the Atlantic. In addition, there were three cruise missile/defensive units, a squadron of MiG-21 fighters, forty-eight Ilyushin Il-28 'Beagle' medium-range jet bombers, and two anti-aircraft units. There were also four infantry regiments to guard the missile sites.[2]

The Il-28s were capable of dropping bombs similar to the one that had destroyed Nagasaki in 1945. Their targets were not the American mainland, which they could have

A Soviet R12 medium-range missile, in a parade through Moscow.

easily reached, but the US ships that would, in the event of an invasion, soon be gathering in Cuban waters. The attacking marines and soldiers would be secondary targets.

The spectre of offensive nuclear weapons on Cuba had haunted Kennedy's administration for many months. As early as August 1962, reports from spy networks on the island had told of the presence of the MiG fighters and bombers. U-2 spy planes on their sorties over Cuba photographed surface-to-air missiles at no fewer than eight different sites, their presence indicating to the CIA that the only reason they were on the island was to defend ballistic surface-to-surface weapons. As yet, however, no such missiles had been identified. It was all supposition, and there was no hard evidence to back up the hunches.

As the Soviet build-up proceeded, it was inevitable that the increased activity would be noted by pro-American agents on the island. Getting the missiles to Cuba was merely the first stage in a very difficult process. Unloading them was bad enough; transporting them to the designated launch sites along hillsides and poorly maintained Cuban roads was even worse. Accidents became commonplace as Juanita Castro later recalled:

> As the summer ended, the roads and highways of Cuba throbbed with military traffic. Troops were on the move. Soviet convoys droned day and night. So heavy was the traffic that Cuba was suddenly beset with a rash of accidents – mostly caused by Soviet soldiers driving like madmen in their jeeps.[3]

Despite convoys travelling only at night, and with the transporting soldiers dressed in civilian clothing or Cuban army uniforms, it was a tactic that fooled no one. The soldiers were forbidden to use Russian. They were ordered to talk to each other in what little Spanish they knew. Inevitably, of course, Russian expletives were heard whenever something went wrong, when lorries would not go around the village squares, or when the soldiers thought they were out of the hearing of their officers.

A U-2 aircraft above the clouds.

Decoy convoys were sometimes sent out in opposite directions from the real routes to be taken, while roads and travel routes were sealed off. In some instances, Soviet engineers cut down telegraph poles or even built new roads around some of the smaller towns and villages.

This was no minor affair. Despite the elaborate security arrangements, however, everyone knew that something big was happening. Soon hundreds of reports were flooding into the CIA offices at Langley. The reports were not always reliable, and those that were, seemed only to confirm Soviet claims that the weapons were of a purely defensive nature. One or two, however, were more alarming.

These spoke of long, cylindrical objects being transported on huge carriers, so big that they could not make all of the turns on the winding Cuban roads. Often the lorries had to back up and make several attempts to get round corners in the villages. It seemed to hint of missiles considerably larger than the defensive anti-aircraft weapons that the Soviets had already admitted sending.

In all, the Soviet intention was to construct nine missile-launch sites: six for the R12s and three for the larger R14s. That would eventually locate forty missile launchers on the island.

At the end of September, US naval reconnaissance aircraft identified several Ilyushin light bombers on the deck of the transport *Kasimov*, which was steaming towards Cuba. With the surface-to-air missiles on the island arranged in what the US military called 'typical Russian fashion', nobody could deny increased Soviet involvement. Kennedy's administration tightened its collective breath and promptly passed control of the U-2 flights from the CIA to the air force.

The government was still troubled by the loss of a U-2 spy plane, piloted by Gary Powers, in 1960. Kennedy and his advisors did not care to revisit the political ramifications of that. It was felt that, in the event of further U-2 losses, air force ownership of a downed U-2 could be better explained than one operated by an intelligence agency like the CIA.

Despite counselling restraint during these early days of the crisis, Kennedy was under considerable pressure from Republicans as well as from Democrats in marginal seats. Congress was adamant that it wanted a strong military response to the posturing of Castro and Khrushchev. Pressure also came from the Joint Chiefs of Staff:

'Virtually his entire national security apparatus was pushing the President to take military action against Cuba.'[4]

Kennedy resisted. He and his colleagues spent hours in discussion, trying hard to broker a deal that would please both sides of the argument. Perhaps his wisest advisors – and certainly the least belligerent – were his brother Bobby, his speech writer Ted Sorensen, and Defense Secretary Robert McNamara. All of them advocated 'holding fire', at least for the moment.

Arthur Schlesinger summed up Kennedy's attitude and thoughts when he wrote that, if the Bay of Pigs fiasco had taught the president anything, it was to distrust the Joint Chiefs of Staff and their warlike recommendations. Despite the tense situation, and with a surprising degree of bitter humour, Kennedy himself declared, 'These brass hats have one

Ted Sorensen, advisor and
speech writer for JFK.

great advantage in their favour. If we do what they want us to do, none of us will be alive
later to tell them that they were wrong.'[5]

If Kennedy and his staff were pondering the future, so too were Khrushchev and his
colleagues in Moscow. It was, they knew, a dangerous game of brinkmanship they were
playing, not just for the USSR, but also for their leader, a man who had previously sought
peaceful co-existence with the West, but was now bringing the world close to the brink of
a nuclear holocaust. Yet once that bluff and brinkmanship had started there was no easy
way to climb down.

As if to prove the point, a letter from Khrushchev to Kennedy – in the days before
the 'hot line' and the instant communications of the twenty-first century – received on
28 September, made things totally clear: 'An American attack on Cuba would bring retali-
atory action against Berlin.'[6]

The matter could not have been spelled out any better. The threat was not just to mainland USA. It was also directed at the civilian population of West Berlin.

5. DISCOVERY

The renewal of reconnaissance flights over Cuba was authorized on 9 October, but bad weather kept the U-2 spy planes grounded for several days. The pilots of these single-seat reconnaissance aircraft were forced to kick their heels and wait. Five days later, the skies were clear and the spying operations could recommence.

On the morning of Sunday, 14 October, a U-2, flown by Major Richard Heyser, spent just six minutes over the island, but in that time 928 images were taken. Heyser, already a veteran of the Korean War and soon to fly combat missions in Vietnam, was piloting a U-2 remodelled for in-flight refuelling. The aircraft had recently been taken over from the CIA. As part of the transfer, the paint job was brand new and the aircraft was now recorded as USAF 66675.[1]

Heyser's mission, irreverently dubbed 'Brass Nob', involved him flying at a height of 72,500ft above the island. His greatest threat was likely to come from the Russian SAM missiles. In fact, he encountered no opposition, despite having been within range of SAM anti-aircraft batteries for ten minutes. He was soon once more over the Florida coast, landing at McCoy Air Base, close to Orlando, to pass across the photographs for developing.

The images were studied by experts at the CIA's National Photographic Interpretation Centre. The heart-stopping conclusion was that the Soviets were in the process of installing launch sites for both R12 and R14 medium-range ballistic missiles. These were certainly not ground-to-air missiles. These were weapons capable of hitting targets well inside the Atlantic coast of America. Four of the missile sites were already operational.[2]

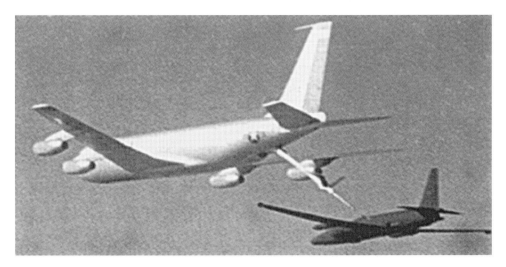

A U2-F refuels while airborne, a development and modification that gave the high-level reconnaissance aircraft even greater range.

Major Richard Heyser, fourth from left in the back row, in a group view of U-2 pilots who were instrumental in discovering the missiles on Cuba.

Now the words of Cuban President Osvaldo Dorticos at the United Nations a week earlier made sudden sense. Dorticos's position as president of Cuba was a nominal role, the man being little more than a figurehead under Castro but, even so, Dorticos's voice was significant and clearly worth listening to: 'If we are attacked, we will defend ourselves. I repeat, we have sufficient means with which to defend ourselves; we have, indeed ... weapons which we would have preferred not to acquire and which we do not wish to employ.'[3]

Obviously, in a rather oblique and mysterious way, Dorticos was referring to the Soviet missiles, something that did not become obvious until Heyser's photographs were developed.

The CIA photographic experts had made their judgements, partly from studying the U-2 images and partly from information provided by Colonel Oleg Penkovsky, a Russian double-agent working for Britain's MI6 and the CIA. Penkovsky's betrayal of his country – although many believe that he was also working for Soviet military intelligence, a real triple-cross – is a story worthy of any John le Carré spy novel.

Penkovsky's reports over the years prior to Heyser's photographs had been concerned, largely, with the dimensions of the Soviet missiles and other technical details, including the layout of a typical Russian launch site. This information, combined with the new images, was enough to cause immediate alarm.

Having come to their conclusions, the CIA immediately notified the White House. For some reason, National Security Advisor McGeorge Bundy chose not to tell the president that night, even though Secretary of Defence Robert McNamara was immediately briefed.

National Security Advisor
McGeorge Bundy at the
White House.

Instead, Bundy waited until just after 8.00 am the following morning, 16 October, before knocking on Kennedy's door and announcing the news. Kennedy was still in bed, dressed in pyjamas and dressing gown, reading the morning papers. He was quickly and rudely jolted out of his reverie by Bundy's news.

The president, like most non-military personnel, could make little of the long-distance photographs that Richard Heyser had risked his life to take, but he trusted the professionalism of the analysts. Bobby Kennedy, called immediately to his brother's side, also struggled to identify missiles and other weapons of war.

At 11.45 am that morning, the CIA made a formal presentation of their findings to Kennedy and other senior officials. To Bobby Kennedy, on being told by the CIA experts that what he was looking at was the construction of a missile site at San Cristobal, there was a sense of unreality in the situation:

> I, for one, had to take their word for it. I examined the pictures carefully, and what I saw appeared to be no more than the clearing of a field for a farm or the basement of a house. I was relieved to hear later that this was the same reaction of virtually everyone at the meeting, including President Kennedy. Even a few days later, when more work had taken place on the site, he remarked that it looked like a football field.[4]

The siting of offensive Russian missiles on Cuba was something that everyone had suspected and feared for months. They were a clear danger to the US and to the world.

Determined to avoid a panic, it was decided to keep the information as secret as possible, at least for the moment. As part of this ploy, Kennedy stuck rigidly to his schedule of public appearances and meetings for much of the morning of the 16th. These included

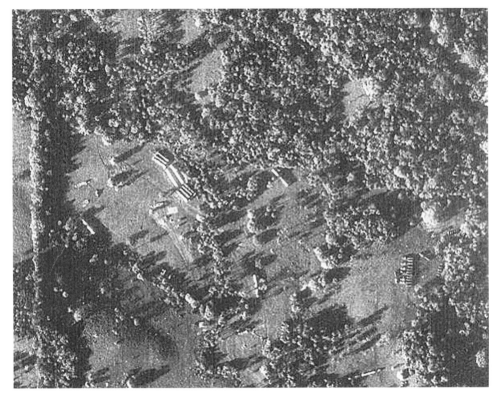

One of Heyser's aerial photographs. Bobby Kennedy and JFK thought it resembled a football field or the clearing of a field to make a barn.

chairing a conference on mental-health issues and meeting various dignitaries. He finally managed to extricate himself from what must have been an excruciating programme of events in time for his 11.45 am meeting with the CIA.

President Kennedy appeared to be exceptionally calm, but inside he was fuming, not least at himself for being taken in by Khrushchev. He had, he felt, been duped and once again treated like a fool by the Soviet premier, but knew that he could not respond with a knee-jerk reaction. That way there lay war with both the USSR and Cuba.

At the same time, he asked himself, was the option of doing nothing a viable or realistic course of action? In the Cold War climate of bluff and brinkmanship, could he simply stand by and allow the USSR to tweak his nose, singe his beard, or whatever metaphor he cared to conjure? The president had a lot to think about. In the meantime, not least of which was to continue with the U-2 reconnaissance flights.

At 6.30 pm on the evening of 16 October, Kennedy convened the first meeting of a totally new committee, something that was coined the Executive Committee of the National Security Council. Consisting of nine members of the Security Council, plus five other co-opted advisors, the group was known as EXCOMM.

EXCOMM meeting, 29 October 1962. Discussion was intense, but Bobby Kennedy, extreme left, appeared bored.

Other notables like Adlai Stevenson also attended meetings from time to time on an ad hoc basis. It was a group that held the fate of the world in its hands and was to meet every day until the crisis was finally ended, thirteen days later.

Unknown to the members of EXCOMM, Kennedy arranged to have all meetings of the group secretly recorded. With these tapes recently released and made public, it is clear that the debates and discussions between members were often heated. Members vacillated between one position and the next, and the thread of uncertainty was clearly apparent.

Part of the problem facing EXCOMM lay in the fact that there was no effective response plan in place. Kennedy's administration had felt that the Soviets would never be so foolish as to locate surface-to-surface missiles on Cuba. This vacuum, allowed the Chiefs of Staff to keep pushing for military action, long before the presence of offensive Soviet missiles on the island was discovered.

As their meetings settled into a regular routine, the members of EXCOMM discussed their options. They had a whole range of them to consider.

They could do nothing and simply hope the problem would go away. As a plan, however, it was never realistic, as Castro was too unpredictable to be left with weapons of mass destruction, and the thought of effectively allowing him to launch these missiles whenever he felt slighted, was too much to bear. Apart from anything else, American pride could not acknowledge that they had been outwitted by Khrushchev and Castro. Option one – out.

The possibility of using shadowy diplomacy was considered. This basically came down to threats, offering Castro a choice: get rid of the missiles or risk a US invasion. Threats had never worked with the Cuban leader in the past, and now, with the missiles in place, such an approach was even more unlikely to succeed. Option two – out.

Taking the matter to the United Nations or other diplomatic channels and pressurizing Khrushchev to remove the missiles was also felt to be a blind alley that led only to humiliation for whichever side backtracked first. Option three – out.

An immediate air-and-ground attack on Cuba and the missile sites was an obvious option. Even McNamara had, initially, been in favour of an assault. OPLAN 312 (air attack) and OPLAN 316 (invasion) were drawn up by the Joint Chiefs of Staff and were discussed on many occasions. Only the president could order the attacks to begin – much to the chagrin of the military – and for the time being, Kennedy chose not to take this course of action. Option Four – maybe.

In the end, EXCOMM found itself left with a limited choice of responses. One, launch a full-scale invasion of Cuba. Two, use US aircraft to attack and destroy all the known missile sites. Three, use the US Navy to blockade Cuba and so prevent the arrival of missiles.

As might be expected, the Joint Chiefs of Staff were in favour of an invasion and a full-scale attack. The Chiefs of Staff made up an impressive group under Chairman General Maxwell Taylor. It consisted of Curtis LeMay (air force), George Armstrong (navy), Earle Wheeler (army) and David Shoup (Marine Corps), all with extensive combat experience and all, by nature, always inclined towards the military options.

LeMay, in particular, was convinced that a hard response was called for. In an outburst worthy of General Patton at his most rambunctious, he stated that the missile sites should be bombed, the soldiers of the missile regiments killed. In return, the Russians would do nothing. It was, he believed, the only choice. A blockade of Cuba would do nothing more than revive the spectre of Munich before the Second World War: 'It reeked of cowardly Neville Chamberlain,' he growled.[5]

Kennedy, afraid that his Chiefs of Staff would start a war without his approval, was initially in favour of an air attack on Cuba. General Taylor was clear, however. An air strike might seem the best response but it would never be 100 per cent effective – one suggestion was that at least 10 per cent of the missile sites would survive an assault. That would give the Russians time and opportunity to retaliate by launching strikes against mainland USA.

The question of casualties was also worrying. Taylor estimated that there could be as many as 18,500 US casualties in the first ten days of any invasion, and that was without Russian or Cuban use of nuclear weapons.[6] The assault called for 500 sorties by the USAF, targeting missile sites and airfields, followed within a few days by marine and army landings. Such an action could begin, Kennedy was informed, on 23 October.

Kennedy, after prolonged discussion with Bobby, Sorensen and McNamara, began to change his mind and move away from the idea of an all-out attack on Cuba. He did not, as yet, know which alternative option he would choose, but he was, by instinct, appalled by the consequences of military action.

General Curtis LeMay, fourth from left, and a group of U-2 pilots meet the president.

NUCLEAR WARHEAD BUNKER
UNDER CONSTRUCTION
SAN CRISTOBAL SITE 1

PREFABRICATION MATERIALS

Nuclear warhead bunker under construction at San Cristobal.

Air strikes alone were not the answer. Everyone knew they would have to be followed by an invasion. Thousands of American troops charging the beaches would inevitably mean many casualties, American, Russian and Cuban. Equally as worrying to Kennedy was the thought that, even if attacks on Cuba were successful, the Soviets still had the ability to move against Berlin. There was, clearly, no easy solution.

When EXCOMM was informed that the warheads for the Cuban missiles were not yet in place, there was a slight drop in tension. Secretary for Defense Robert McNamara was suddenly aware that the president had been given time in which to make a decision. There was time, also, for a little humour. General David M. Shoup, commander of the Marine Corps, summed up everyone's feelings: 'You're in a pretty bad fix, Mr President.'

The president answered quickly, 'If I am you are in it with me.'

Everyone laughed, and with no final decision, the meeting was adjourned.[7]

McNamara, Sorensen and Bobby Kennedy had, by now, come down in favour of a blockade. They were facing an intense lobby from the Chiefs of Staff and people like former Secretary of State Dean Acheson, all of whom believed that the president had a responsibility, not just to the American people, but to the rest of the world as well; a responsibility that culminated in just one thing – the destruction of the missiles.

Much of the debate centred on the moral question of launching an assault that would, apart from military casualties, kill thousands of innocent civilians, something that neither the Kennedys nor McNamara found particularly palatable. There was also the matter of the strategic balance of power in the world. While the Chiefs of Staff believed that the presence of Soviet missiles in Cuba would alter this, McNamara, in particular, took the opposite view.

With the strategic warheads of the USA outnumbering the Soviets' by almost twenty to one, the addition of an extra forty in Cuba would, McNamara felt, make no difference. And yet, although the number of Cuban missiles mattered little, Kennedy could not afford to allow the USSR to change the political and strategic balance of power. Therefore, the US had to be seen to act, particularly as 'appearances contribute to reality'.[8]

Khrushchev had no suspicion that the presence of the offensive missile sites had been discovered – and Kennedy was determined to keep it that way. In a meeting with Russian Minister of Foreign Affairs Andrei Gromyko on 18 October, he allowed the Russian to continue with the standard line of denial that had been the Soviet tactic all along.

In the meantime, rather than alert the Cubans and the Soviets to the fact that the missile sites had been discovered, the U-reconnaissance operations over Cuba continued. It was not just part of the deception; there was also the possibility that more information could be gleaned by the flights.

President Kennedy did his best to retain an appearance of normality over the next few days. While EXCOMM continued to meet, Kennedy, who must have been in a turmoil of anger, uncertainty and frustration, had to make a show of going about his duties. On Saturday, 20 October, he was out of Washington on a two-day campaign tour of the Midwest when a telephone call from his brother summoned him back to the White House. There was deadlock among the advisors and the president, finally, had to make a decision.

The president has a cold, press and campaign organizers were told, and has to cancel his scheduled meetings and engagements. It fooled no one. While Kennedy was bundled into the relative comfort of Air Force One, the press pack fought to find their own transport to follow him back to the nation's capital.

By now the options had come down to two: an air strike or a blockade. While Kennedy was leaning towards the blockade, he had not completely made up his mind. Worryingly,

When President Kennedy met Soviet Minister for Foreign Affairs Andrei Gromyko on 18 October 1962 he did not disclose that the US knew about the missiles.

news of the danger from Cuba was almost out in the public domain. EXCOMM had so far managed to avoid major leaks, but insistent investigative reporters were now closer to the truth than they ever imagined. Kennedy sought advice, from ex-President Eisenhower, among others, but at the end of the day, only he could decide what to do.

When, on Monday, 22 October, all non-military personnel were evacuated from the Guantanamo Bay Naval Base on Cuba, rumours ran rife. The evacuation was accompanied by the arrival of large detachments of US Marines. Ed Buler, a 39-year-old naval commander, based at Guantanamo as commanding officer of a training squadron, saw the new arrivals: 'Planeloads of US Marines, fresh from California, squinting in the tropical sunshine. "Are we in Hawaii?" they asked. No, we told them. It's the other end of the world.'[9]

Buler, like his compatriots, was not scared by the situation, especially once he took his aircraft high above Cuba and saw the fleet of carriers and destroyers ranged off the island. Nobody in their right mind, he thought, was ever going to challenge such a show of strength. Nevertheless, there was still the evacuation to manage. When he went to find his wife, she was on the first tee of the golf course: 'I couldn't yell out that we were going to have an evacuation because they weren't supposed to know yet. So I had to stand there while she went off to get her golf ball.'[10]

Faced by the spectre of lurid headlines in the morning newspapers, Kennedy was reluctantly forced to telephone the publishers of the country's two major papers, the *New York Times* and *The Washington Post*, to ask them to hold off on the story for a day or so. The two papers did as they were asked, but in Europe there was no such restriction. On the

MILITARY CAMPS, REMEDIOS AREA, CUBA
25 OCTOBER 1962

A military camp at Remedios, one of many similar U2 photographs.

morning of 22 October, many of the dailies ran with the story of potential war between the USA and the Soviet Union out in the Caribbean.

Importantly, the president, while taking advice from EXCOMM and people like his brother Bobby, remained the sole arbiter in the decision-making process. Even Congress was kept in the dark: 'Congress remained ignorant of the Soviet missiles in Cuba during the first week of EXCOMM deliberations. Only on October 22, two hours before his broadcast to the world, did the President assemble the leaders of both houses [and] advise them of the missiles.'[11]

By now several of the EXCOMM members had tempered their opinions in favour of the blockade. By the Monday morning, Kennedy had made his decision. The USA would implement a naval blockade of Cuba – a quarantine as Kennedy preferred to call it – in order to prevent Soviet missiles reaching the island. That evening he would address the American people and explain the situation. After that the press could write whatever they liked.

6. ADDRESSING THE NATIONS

Kennedy had made his decision on the basis of two important facts. Firstly, an air attack could not be certain of taking out every single one of the Cuban missiles and, secondly, nobody could reassure him that an air assault would not destroy America's moral standing in the world.[1] This last reason was a major factor in all of Kennedy's decisions and actions during the missile crisis.

His decision was not without its critics both in EXCOMM and in Congress, not least because there were already missiles on Cuba and the imposition of a blockade was arguably a case of shutting the door after the horse had bolted. There was also the possibility that, faced with a blockade, the Soviets might rush to complete the instillation of those missiles already available to them. Then, if the blockade failed to persuade Khrushchev to remove the weapons, the US might still have to launch air attacks, but now against missiles that were active and operational.

Disaster was closer than anyone thought. The U-2 flights had revealed the presence of the R12 missile sites, but they had not discovered the presence of 100 short-range battlefield missiles that would undoubtedly be used against any invading force. Apart from death and destruction on the beaches, the results could have wider implications as radiation fallout from these battlefield missiles might well be carried by prevailing winds to both Havana and the Florida coast. Amazingly, the presence of these short-range tactical missiles was never discovered. The US did not find out about them until 2002.

Meanwhile, Adlai Stevenson came up with the alternative suggestion that Khrushchev should be told that the US would withdraw the missiles recently installed in Turkey – something that clearly upset the Soviets – if he would be prepared to remove the missiles on Cuba. Stevenson also felt that the base at Guantanamo Bay should be returned to the Cubans.

Kennedy rejected the proposal, although he, too, was unsure about the

Veteran diplomat and politician Adlai Stevenson.

value of the Jupiter missiles in Turkey. The presence of these weapons, so close to the Russian border, had been a major factor in guiding Khrushchev's actions, but to openly suggest their removal now would be like backing down before the bully's fists. As for Guantanamo Bay, there was no way it would be abandoned while the Soviet threat was real and alive.

In 2010, Sergei Khrushchev, son of former premier Nikita, was asked how much the presence of those missiles contributed to his father's actions with regard to Cuba. His answer was emphatic: 'Zero. The missiles in Turkey were the same as the missiles in Italy and Great Britain. Why do you make the difference between those missile bases? They are the same.'[2]

Whether or not Sergei was defending his father's reputation, at the height of the Cold War nothing was straightforward. Both Khrushchev and Kennedy were looking for bargaining tools. While the Jupiters were out of date, their significance cannot be underplayed. They were an expendable asset or threat, depending on which side you came from.

The idea of a blockade was not straightforward, either. According to International Law, the imposition of any blockade was an open act of war. Admiral Anderson, 'Gorgeous George' as he was known, had moved from his initial warlike stance and, for the time being at least, was backing Kennedy. He wrote that America did not want to prohibit all materiel going to the island. Rather, the tactic would be used to prevent only nuclear weapons reaching Cuba. Hence the less belligerent term 'quarantine'.

At Kennedy's direction, the State Department, operating at great haste, appealed for support to the Organization of American States (the OAS) and, on 23 October, received an almost unanimous vote. As long as the quarantine took place in international waters, there would be no problem.

Several Latin American countries now began to offer help for the quarantine operation. Argentina sent two destroyers and made a submarine and a battalion of marines available if needed. Venezuela, Trinidad and Tobago also offered help in the shape of warships and repair facilities.[3]

The actual presence of these ships mattered little, as the US already possessed the largest and most powerful navy in the world. It was the support of the Latin American nations that was most significant, the establishing of a solidarity that would be bound to disturb and perhaps isolate Khrushchev and Castro.

The support and acquiescence of America's allies in Europe and elsewhere were also solicited. France gave rapid approval, President De Gaulle nodding his agreement without even seeing the U-2 images. Konrad Adenauer of West Germany and John Diefenbaker of Canada were equally as helpful. However, perhaps the greatest support for Kennedy and his administration came from Britain.

British Prime Minister Harold MacMillan had already established a close relationship with Kennedy. MacMillan, whose mother was American, had spent some time as minister-resident at Eisenhower's HQ in North Africa during the Second World War, where he had become fond of the Americans he had met. He was always inclined to favour the USA in any dealings he might have.

In an almost paternalistic way, he thought very highly of Kennedy, and on several occasions during the crisis he gave him advice over the telephone. For his part, Kennedy was happy to listen to the counsel of the older and more experienced politician.

While MacMillan advised caution, he was aware that the creation of missile sites on Cuba had changed medium-range rockets into lethal weapons of war that could strike at almost any part of the USA. More importantly, he knew that Kennedy had to do something about it. He would do everything he could to assist, including the help of Britain's V-bomber squadrons. To Air Vice-Marshal Michael Robinson, it was all quite clear. America was nothing if not pragmatic about the situation and the help that allies might give: 'When you have something to offer, they are interested. What we had to offer was Geography. We were like an off-shore aircraft carrier.'[4]

As a result, Bomber Command was placed on alert.

Vulcan bombers of the RAF. (Photo MoD)

The Vulcans, Valiants and Victors, which made up the V-bomber squadrons were, at that stage, the cutting edge of Britain's nuclear deterrent. Control and use of nuclear weapons later passed to the navy with their Polaris submarines but in 1962, it rested firmly on the shoulders of the RAF. In the words of Marshal of the Air Force Sir Michael Beetham: 'MacMillan said that he wanted Bomber Command to take all measures without alarming the general public and that is how we operated.'[5]

All that was now left was for Kennedy to make his televised address to the American nation. This took place at 7.00 pm on the evening of 22 October, the live speech coming from the Oval Office in the White House.

The address began in the usual fashion: 'Good evening, my fellow citizens.' It ended with a clear indication of what he and his government wanted to achieve: 'Peace and freedom, here in this Hemisphere, and we hope, around the world.'

In between, Kennedy went into as much detail as the situation allowed:

The Government, as promised, has maintained the closest surveillance of the Soviet military build-up on the island of Cuba. Within the past week unmistakeable evidence has established the fact that a series of offensive missile sites is now in preparation on that imprisoned island. The purposes of these bases can be none other than to provide a nuclear strike capability against the Western Hemisphere.[6]

President Kennedy signs the order to implement the quarantine of Cuba.

The American people had been warned, by constant news flashes, that the president was going to make an important announcement, and millions of them tuned in to hear Kennedy's words that night. Staring directly into the camera, Kennedy was serious but confident, as he outlined the damage that the missiles could inflict. He explained the US response to the situation: 'To halt this offensive build-up, a strict quarantine on all offensive military equipment under shipment to Cuba is being initiated. All ships of any kind bound for Cuba from whatever nation or port will, if found to contain cargoes of offensive weapons, be turned back.'[7]

He moved on to appeal to Khrushchev to stop 'this clandestine, reckless and provocative threat to world peace' before issuing a thinly veiled threat of his own: 'Any hostile move anywhere in the world against the safety and freedom of peoples to whom we are committed – including in particular the brave people of West Berlin – will be met by whatever action is needed.'[8]

The reaction to Kennedy's speech was, in the main, positive. Nobody wanted war, but most people felt that, in the circumstances, the president was doing the best he could. There were some, notably Republicans, who wanted a more forceful response, but with the spectre of nuclear destruction hovering overhead, the majority of the nation felt that their young president had done well. Ray Dalton's opinion was typical of many Americans:

I was still in High School, living in Lauderdale, which is pretty damned close to Cuba. I reckoned if anything started we were bound to get it first. I remember sitting in front of the TV set with my family, watching Kennedy's broadcast. I was young, caught up with it all and I reckoned he'd done brilliantly.

'Not bad,' said my father, 'but not a patch on FDR with his Day of Infamy after Japan had bombed Pearl Harbour.'

My mom looked at him and shrugged. She was English. She'd met dad when he was in England during the war and came back home with him. A GI bride, that's what she was called.

Anyway, she said that Kennedy and Roosevelt could both take a hike. 'You want a really good message to the people, listen to Churchill – we will fight them on the beaches and all that stuff.'

They went on and on. I just let them argue. I thought, and I still think, that Kennedy's talk was about right at a time of national crisis. Let war come, I thought, we'll teach the Ruskies a lesson.[9]

The US Strategic Air Command had already gone to what was known as DEFCON 3 (Defence Readiness Condition Three,) with squadrons of fighters and the bomber fleet armed with nuclear weapons. The powerful B-52 bombers were ready to take to the air at just fifteen minutes' notice.

The lessons of Pearl Harbor had been learned. Rather than face an initial Soviet attack, which could take out dozens of aircraft in one hit, the Vought F-8 Crusaders,

Boeing B-47 Stratojets and other US aircraft were dispersed to various airfields across the country. In addition, the army was now also on full alert. Hundreds of men had already been moved to Florida, Georgia and other states on the eastern seaboard.

Copies of Kennedy's speech had been given to the Soviet ambassador in Washington and to Khrushchev, via the Russian foreign ministry, an hour before the president went on television. It was a diplomatic nicety but, more importantly, showed that the USA was still open for communication and discussion.

Castro had been informed that non-combatants were being removed from the Guantanamo base and that US Marine reinforcements were being shipped in. When he heard that Kennedy was about to broadcast to the nation, he knew that the crisis had escalated to a higher level. That was exactly how he was meant to feel.

Through a number of long-distance transmitters based around Miami, and pointed directly at Havana, the US had ensured that Kennedy's broadcast would be seen and heard by Castro and by all Cubans who had TV sets or radios – even by those who did not. All over the island, in towns and villages, in isolated farm houses, and in cities like Havana, dozens of people gathered together to listen to the broadcast, as the Americans knew they would. For these Cubans, Kennedy had a special message:

> Now your leaders are no longer Cuban leaders inspired by Cuban ideals. They are puppets and agents of an international conspiracy which has turned Cuba against your friends and neighbours in the Americas – and turned it into the first Latin American country to become a target for nuclear war, the first Latin American country to have these weapons on its soil.[10]

Castro's response was to be expected. Kennedy had stated that the quarantine was an 'initial response', so nobody knew what America's next move might be. Therefore quick action was required.

He immediately mobilized militiamen and reservists, enlarging his army to around 300,000 men. They may well have been poorly armed, many of them being just teenage boys, but there was no mistaking their enthusiasm or the sheer weight of numbers they brought to the defence of Cuba. Plans laid many months before had split the island into three military commands. Castro's brother Raúl took command of the eastern section, Che Guevara the west, and Juan Almeida, the army Chief of Staff, the central. All of them prepared for immediate action.

Castro remained in Havana. Within a few hours of Kennedy's speech, he was making his own address to the Cuban nation. Unlike the Americans, he had only limited access to his people through radio or television. In the USA, these implements of 'new media' were a means of universal communication. Here on the island, with TV and radio ownership just a fraction of what it was in America, it was much more 'hit or miss'.

What Castro did have was newspapers, in particular the highly supportive *Revolución*, which had been behind him since his days as a guerrilla fighter in the jungles and hills of the island. The papers were always eagerly read by the Cubans and now was the time to make them a direct statement.

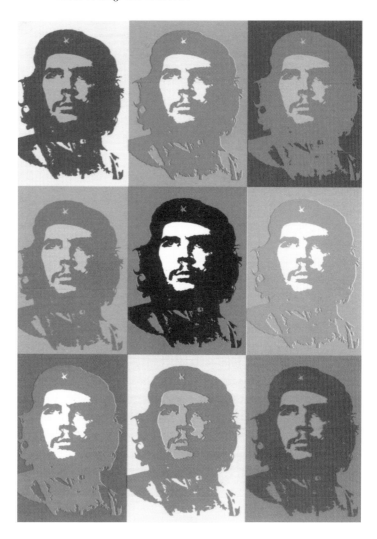

Guevara – all part of
creating the legend.

At the paper's offices in the capital Castro directed and dictated the news he wanted displayed on the front page the next morning. He paced the newsroom with an almost frenetic energy, but he remained, at all times, in control of his emotions – something he did not always manage to achieve.

If Kennedy's broadcast had presented him as serious, analytical and studied, Fidel's response was the exact opposite. Using the rhetoric and bravado for which he was famous, he made his appeal directly to the hearts of the Cubans. It was the approach they wanted from their leader. It was part of the reason he was always called Fidel by his people, rather than the formal Castro that the international press used:

The nation has woken up on a war footing, ready to repulse any attack. Every weapon is in its place, and beside each weapon are the heroic defenders of the Revolution and

59

the Motherland ... From the length and breadth of the island resounds like thunder, from millions of voices, with more fervour and reason than ever before, the historic and glorious cry 'Motherland or Death'.[11]

To coincide with the publication of the paper, the following morning Castro appeared on Cuban television. Limited as it was, with perhaps one in fifty people on the island owning a TV set, he knew that the paper headlines would have alerted his countrymen and that the word would quickly get around: Fidel is on television. Then, as with Kennedy's broadcast the previous night, they would gather round the one television set in the village and listen with rapt attention.

Castro was a brilliant public speaker. Like Trotsky and Hitler before him, he knew exactly how to grab his audience, starting slowly, quietly, almost inaudibly, before rising to a full-throated scream of indignation. If necessary, and if the topic inspired him, he would talk for hours. Today, his words were both stirring and captivating. Referring to Kennedy's throw-away comment that the Cubans were 'a captive people', Castro was both scathing and dramatic: 'He is talking about a people that have hundreds of thousand men under arms. He should have said the armed captive people of Cuba.'[12]

Castro spoke for an hour and a half, then promptly leapt out of his chair and left the TV studio. It was stage craft of the highest order. To those watching it was as if he had quit the safety of Havana, and left to join Che and the others at the battle front.

Che Guevara, at the western end of the island, held the position closest to the USA. If the Americans came, they would surely land here, he felt. He welcomed the challenge. It was more to his liking than looking after the economy of the island, a task that Castro had given him following the revolution in 1959. The implementation of Marxist ideals had proved difficult, if not impossible. Revolution and combat were things he understood well, so let the Americans come.

Nikita Khrushchev had begun to suspect that the missiles had been detected even before he was given a copy of Kennedy's speech. There had lately been a great deal of activity around the White House, and large troop movements, such as those conducted in the southern states of the USA, were bound to draw his attention. The fact that Kennedy was about to speak to the American people, on a matter of some urgency, merely added to his unease.

The Cuban missiles were a threat rather than simply weapons of war. If everything had gone according to plan, with the launching sites completed and missiles and warheads installed, there was little that the Americans could have done. Now, however, the Soviet premier found himself caught on the horns of a dilemma. He and the members of the Presidium – effectively the spearhead of the Communist Party – discussed the options at length.

By now, Soviet warheads had arrived, the first shipment for R12 rockets being unloaded on 4 October. Just prior to Kennedy's broadcast and the imposition of the quarantine, twenty-four one-megaton warheads for the R14 rockets had also been delivered. Armageddon loomed closer.

Defence Minister Rodion Malinovsky was in favour of allowing Soviet troops to use whatever means were necessary to defend Cuba. Khrushchev was opposed to the idea. Such an order would allow the men *in situ* to fire the MRBMs, and that would undoubtedly be the beginning of a nuclear war.

Like Kennedy, Khrushchev had several options open to him. He could announce a defence treaty with Cuba, arguably something that should have been done before the missiles had arrived on the island. This would give him carte blanche to provide Castro with weapons, in the way that the USA had armed Turkey. Or he could pass ownership and control of the missiles to Castro, then bow out of the danger zone. Alternatively, he could simply wait for an American invasion and then use the missiles to hit the USA. What to do?

When he finally read Kennedy's speech, Khrushchev's immediate reaction was one of relief. The US president was not declaring all-out war, but simply announcing a blockade, along with the demand that the missiles on Cuba be removed. There was, Khrushchev noticed, no deadline for the removal.

He told the Presidium members that, while three R12 missile regiments, along with their weapons, were already on the island, many of the R14s were still at sea and now, due to Kennedy's quarantine, were highly unlikely to reach their destination. It would, he felt, be better to turn the ships around rather than risk a face-to-face with blockading US warships.

Despite objections from Malinovsky and others, orders were issued on 23 October for fourteen ships, which were probably carrying Soviet R14 missiles and equipment, to reverse course and return to port. Other vessels closer to Cuba and already inside the quarantine line, carrying warheads and R14 missiles, were allowed to proceed. The four Foxtrot-class submarines, hidden in the depths of the ocean, presented Khrushchev with a problem he could not yet solve.

Eventually, it was decided to hold back the Foxtrots for a day or so, rather than have them try to negotiate the area around the southern Bahamas and the Turks and Caicos Islands. The American anti-submarine patrols would be bound to detect them in such shallow waters and the threat of confrontation was very real. Wait and see what happens was the tactic, nobody yet realizing that the detection of one of the Foxtrots would soon bring the world closer to war than it had ever been.

On 23 October, American Crusader jets, led by William Ecker, the CO of Photo Reconnaissance Squadron 62, thundered over the island at a height of under 500ft.

Ecker's photographs were much sharper and more distinct than Major Heyser's original U-2 images, which had been taken from high altitude. These new photographs showed that work on the missile sites had proceeded apace. It was estimated that the launching pads and the missiles themselves would be ready for war within a few days. Khrushchev, it was believed, clearly had no intention of backing down.

Khrushchev had quickly dismissed the idea of a defence treaty with Cuba, as well as the notion of handing control of the missiles over to Castro. Instead, he issued a direct order to his commanders on Cuba, stating that they were to resist any attempt at invasion

An F-8 Crusader jet.

by American troops, but not to use nuclear weapons. Approval for their use could only come from him.

That night, on Khrushchev's command, the Soviet leaders slept in the Kremlin. Like Kennedy keeping up his formal engagements, it was done so as not to cause alarm among the Russian people by the constant movement of high officials from the Presidium. It must have been an uncomfortable night for all concerned, trying to sleep on office chairs and sofas.

As the leader of a totalitarian regime, Khrushchev saw no need to broadcast to the Russian people, but in a letter to Kennedy, dated 23 October, he accused the US of 'outright banditry or, if you like, the folly of degenerate imperialism'.[13]

The American press, now fully informed of the situation, took the opposite view. On 24 October, many of them led with headlines on the likely confrontation between American and Soviet ships: 'Soviet vessels bound for the Communist-ruled island steamed towards a US armada posted to enforce the quarantine – and a possible Cold War showdown.'[14]

On the evening of the same day, the Soviet News Agency TASS broadcast to the world that the Soviet Union viewed the blockade as an act of aggression and ships travelling to Cuba would be instructed to ignore it. It was bluff and brinkmanship yet again.

Kennedy responded on 25th, informing the Soviet premier that he had been forced into taking this action after being repeatedly told that no offensive missiles were being placed on Cuba, and then discovering that the Russian assurances were lies. The quarantine would remain.

7. BEYOND DIPLOMACY

On 25 October, with the US requesting an emergency meeting of the Security Council of the United Nations, tensions remained high. The atmosphere within the Security Council that day was electric, all members realizing the seriousness of the situation.

When Adlai Stevenson challenged Valerian Zorin, the Soviet ambassador, to admit the presence of Russian missiles on Cuba, Zorin refused to give a direct answer, stating that the US would receive a reply in due course. Stevenson declared that he would wait 'until Hell freezes over' and then retaliated by displaying Heyser's and Ecker's photographs of the partially built missile sites.

The US quarantine had gone into operation at 10.00 am the day before. As it stood on that taut and tense Wednesday morning, it looked as if face-to-face confrontation and conflict between the two superpowers were not far away.

The exclusion line had originally been drawn at 800 miles off Cuba, meaning that there would soon be contact between the American warships and the foremost Russian transports, which were already perilously close. The line had been set at 800 miles so as to remain outside the range of MiG fighters stationed on the island but, following advice and

Adlai Stevenson displays the US reconnaissance photographs to the United Nations Security Council.

discussion with, among others, British Ambassador David Ormsby-Gore, Kennedy agreed to shorten the quarantine to just 500 miles.[1] That, at least, gave time for further consideration.

Across the world, newspapers and television trumpeted news of Kennedy's actions. Close to home, *The Florida Times-Union* was quick to agree with Kennedy's actions with the headline 'Cuba Action is Applauded by Residents'. The residents in question were from the military and naval city of Jacksonville in northern Florida: 'Jacksonville reacted with wholehearted support to President Kennedy's firm action against the offensive build-up in Cuba by the Soviet Union.'[2]

Under the banner headline 'Blockade', and a sub-headline that declared, 'Ultimatum to Khrushchev "Move Those Missiles"', the British tabloid *Daily Sketch* was relatively low key and informative: 'President Kennedy last night announced a full-scale blockade of Cuba to stop the build-up of Russian missiles there. He said that Cuba had been turned into an offensive base able to rocket destruction into the heart of America.'[3]

The Observer was rather more downbeat in its response, but left everyone in no doubt about what should happen next. In a leader article on Sunday, 28 October, the paper gave this reaction to the way President Kennedy had handled things so far: 'On the whole he showed courage and moderation. But if he wants to retain the support of his allies he must show the same courage and restraint in negotiation.'[4]

If that was a typical English understatement, then there were a number of examples where the traditional British sense of humour came to the fore. Richard Dimbleby, famed TV journalist, signed off that week's current affairs programme *Panorama* with his tongue firmly in his cheek: 'Hopefully we will be with you next Monday, if we haven't in the week all witnessed a very much larger *Panorama*, that is.'[5]

It was truer than Dimbleby knew. It was all very well to lay down a quarantine line, but nobody yet knew what would happen if a Russian vessel refused to stop or if a Soviet captain should happen to refuse the Americans permission to board.

Newspaper headlines from the thirteen days of crisis.

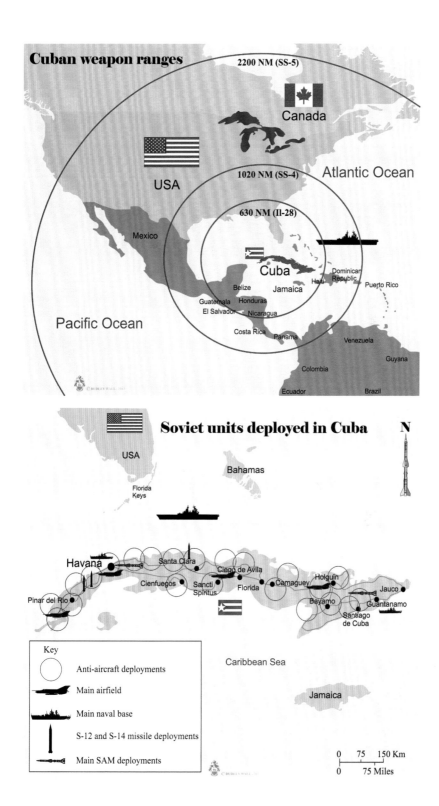

US aircraft deployed during the Cuban Missile Crisis

A-4E Skyhawk of 72 Attack Squadron
(VA-72 Blue Hawks) aboard USS *Independence*

McDonnell RF-101C Voodoo reconnaissance aircraft

Vought F-8C Crusader VF-84 Sqn

Lockheed U-2C

Soviet weapons deployed in Cuba

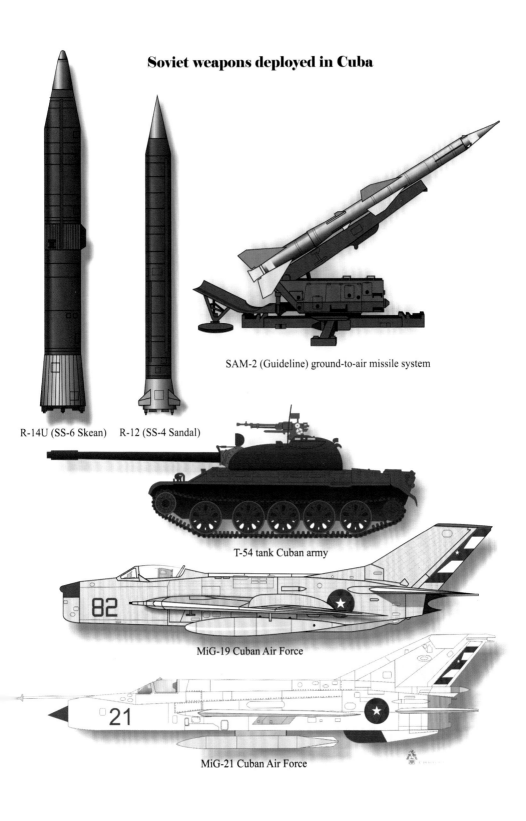

R-14U (SS-6 Skean)   R-12 (SS-4 Sandal)

SAM-2 (Guideline) ground-to-air missile system

T-54 tank Cuban army

MiG-19 Cuban Air Force

MiG-21 Cuban Air Force

USA military insignia of the time

Navy Expeditionary Medal

Armed Forces Expeditionary Medal

The USA authorized the award of two medals for the Cuba Missile Crisis. These were generally awarded to Navy and Marine Corps personnel who served in Cuban waters during the period of tension up to 1962.

The Navy Expeditionary Medal was awarded for service from 3 January 1961 to 23 October 1962.

The Armed Forces Expeditionary Medal was awarded for service from 24 October to the 31 December 1962 to all personnel. Service personnel had to have served in the area latitude 12° to 28° north, and longitude 66° to 84° west.

US Marine Corps cap badge

Army Air Defence Command
shoulder patch 1958 1975

US Navy submariner's qualification badge

Tactical Air Force
patch worn by air force personnel
on flying overalls

USAF Command pilot's qualification wing

US Navy petty officer armourer
(aboard an aircraft carrier)

USAF chest title

Above: Major Rudolf Anderson Memorial, Greenville, South Carolina. (Photo John Foxe)

Below: Bay of Pigs Museum, Cuba. (Photo Alexandra)

Above: Attorney General Robert F. Kennedy, Director of FBI J. Edgar Hoover and President John F. Kennedy. (Photo Cecil William Stoughton)

Below: President John Kennedy, UN Secretary-General U Thant and US ambassador to the UN, Adlai Stevenson, at the Waldorf-Astoria in 1962. (Photo US Government)

Right: Cuban leader
Fidel Castro.

Below: Missile crisis
memorial, Cuba.

Above: McDonnell RF-101C Voodoo, 363rd Tactical Reconnaissance Wing, Shaw Air Force Base. (Photo USAF)

Below: U-2 view from the edge of space at 70,000ft. (Photo Christopher Michel)

What language should be used to hail the Russian ships, people wanted to know? Would the Russians understand English or the Americans Russian? Should the US Navy open fire if a ship refused to stop? There was much to consider and very little time to do it in.

The intention of the blockade was not to board and search all Soviet vessels. Just as Khrushchev had said that the placing of missiles on Cuba was to deter the Americans from invading, so Kennedy hoped that the idea of a blockade would be enough to persuade the Soviets to withdraw the missiles. That hope now appeared to have evaporated, leaving the prospect of a confrontation between American and Soviet ships very real. It was a confrontation that nobody, least of all the US Navy, had much idea as how to handle.

Despite this, the Americans were serious in their intent. The *Western Mail* newspaper, under the banner headline 'Kennedy Blockades Cuba: Russian Ships May be Sunk', reported that: 'A Defence Department spokesman said the United States is prepared to sink Soviet ships, if necessary, to prevent offensive weapons from reaching Cuba.'[6]

The first contact came just after 7.00 am on 25 October. The American carrier USS *Essex* and the destroyer USS *Gearing* tried to intercept and stop the tanker *Bucharest* which was heading for Cuba. The tanker failed to heave to, but was allowed to proceed unhindered as she was clearly carrying no military equipment.

It was hardly an auspicious start to the quarantine. Early the following day, however, the aptly named USS *Joseph P. Kennedy Jr*, a destroyer christened in honour of the

The USS *Essex*, one of several aircraft carriers deployed on ant-submarine patrols.

president's late brother, who had been killed in action in the Second World War, made the first boarding. The *Joseph P. Kennedy Jr* encountered and then stopped the Lebanese freighter *Marucla*. Her cargo was searched, but nothing incriminating was found and the vessel was allowed to sail on.

The US now raised the bar by moving the readiness state from DEFCON 3 to DEFCON 2, just one notch below a declaration of war. It was the only time in American history that such a level of readiness had been imposed.

Twenty-three B-52s, all armed with nuclear weapons, were immediately sent to positions within striking distance of the USSR. They were there not necessarily to attack, but to let the Soviets know the seriousness of US intent.

Tactical Air Command had over 500 aircraft deployed in Florida, but there were problems. With support services strained almost to breaking point, and a severe manpower shortage, it meant that twenty-four reserve squadrons had to be called up, presenting a huge logistical problem. To many it seemed as if the southernmost state in the Union was being overrun by the military. Although the soldiers, aircraft and warships provided a powerful strike force, they were also a superb target for Soviet reprisals or pre-emptive strikes.

On Cuba, there were also difficulties, not with resources, but with relations between Soviet soldiers and the Cuban military: 'The more Soviet material that arrived, the more the Soviets shrouded it in secrecy, refusing to allow Cuban troops to see it, let alone help to unpack and transport it.'[7]

The USS *Joseph P. Kennedy Jr*, named after the president's late brother.

To many of the Cuban officers and troops it seemed as if the Russians simply did not trust their allies, either to keep secret the presence of the missiles or, when the time came, to use them. It was an attitude that led to more than a little tension.

At this stage, the atmosphere in the White House was also extremely brittle. By Friday, 26 October, Kennedy was in a dilemma. The Russians had not wavered or shown any sign of removing the missiles. He was again seriously considering an invasion of Cuba, along with a nuclear strike against the Soviet Union. It was a decision the president delayed, however, in favour of more diplomatic pressure on the USSR.

Low-level flights by F-8 Crusaders were increased from two a day to once every two hours. The Crusaders were flying over the island at treetop level with twin purposes: to take photographs and to reinforce to the Cuban people the strength of the USAF and US Navy. The sudden appearance of the aircraft, so low people felt they could reach out and touch them, certainly disturbed the Cubans, but it did little to shake their resolve.

Throughout the week, communications between the White House and the other involved parties went on daily. Sometimes the exchange of views was open, at other times more clandestine means were needed.

One of the more bizarre of these unofficial moments was a meeting between John Scali of ABC News and Alexander Feklisov, the KGB head of station in Washington. Feklisov, code name Aleksandr Fomin, was the Soviet spy who had received and passed on information he had gleaned about the US atom bomb programme from, among others, the Rosenbergs and Karl Fuchs. The meeting with Scali resulted in the influential American journalist being asked to pass on a proposal.

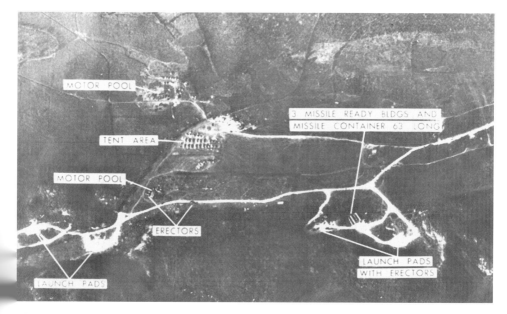

The launch site at Sagua la Grande, 17 October 1962.

Feklisov suggested that the USSR should give an assurance that the missiles on Cuba would be removed, and Castro should publicly state that Cuba would accept no more. In exchange, the USA would announce that it would never launch an invasion of Cuba. Kennedy, when informed, responded to this offer by stating that he did not disregard the proposal, but that the wording would have to be 'the US would be unlikely to ever invade Cuba'.

Kennedy's reply was, at best, a case of semantics but, strangely, the three-part proposal, made quite unofficially by a Soviet spy, was the basis of the deal that was eventually reached. Feklisov duly passed on the information that the would be interested, but his message did not reach Moscow until the Saturday afternoon. In the end, it played no real part in the brokering of a solution.

On Friday, 26 October, at 6.00 pm, the State Department received a message from Khrushchev. It was in the form of a long and rambling letter written by the premier to President Kennedy. It was the second letter from Khrushchev received that day. The first was not made public, but it was a 'softer' version of the second communication, offering to pull the missiles out of Cuba in exchange for a lifting of the quarantine and a pledge never to invade the island. The second letter was a very different, rather strange document: 'There was no question that the letter had been written by him [Khrushchev] personally. It was very long and emotional. But it was not incoherent and the emotion was directed at the death, destruction and anarchy that nuclear war would bring.'[8]

The letter showed that Khrushchev was looking for a way out of the dilemma and was nothing if not placatory: 'We are of sound mind and understand perfectly well that if we attack you, you will respond in the same way. But you too will receive the same that you hurl against us.'[9]

The letter finished with the same offer that had been made by Feklisov earlier in the day, with the addition of a demand that US missiles should be withdrawn from Turkey.

A replica Soviet SS-4 missile on show in Havana. (Photo Suvorow)

The general feeling among the EXCOMM members was that the Feklisov offer had been a preparatory move, designed to 'test the water'. In fact, it was nothing of the sort, Feklisov having been acting on his own initiative.

That same day, 26 October, Castro, with the full support of men like his brother Raúl and Che Guevara, had sent a telegram to Moscow, the 'Armageddon Letter' as it is sometimes known, urging Khrushchev to order a pre-emptive strike against America. Khrushchev shuddered at the demand, and the request was quietly but briskly shelved.

By now Cuba was in tight lockdown, with only military or government vehicles allowed on the roads. Anti-aircraft batteries had been set up along the waterfront in Havana, and Castro ordered that any US aircraft spotted over Cuba was to be fired on. That evening, the CIA reported that the missile sites at San Cristobal and Sagua la Grande were fully operational.

If Khrushchev's letter had seemed to indicate a way out for all concerned, a radio broadcast from Radio Moscow on the morning of 27 October promptly put the Soviet offer into the public domain. The missiles on Cuba would indeed be removed, but only if the US agreed to take their Jupiter missiles out of Turkey:

> You are worried over Cuba. You say that it worries you because it lies at a distance of ninety miles across the sea from the shores of the United States. However, Turkey lies next to us. Our sentinels are pacing up and down and watching each other. Do you believe that you have the right to demand security for your country and the removal of such weapons that you qualify as offensive, while not recognizing this right for us?[10]

The sinister shape of an IL-28. Had a US invasion taken place, this is the aircraft that would have attacked the Marines and the US Navy.

Khrushchev went on to repeat the demand that missiles should be removed from Turkey. Only then would he do the same in Cuba. The Jupiter rockets might be old and unreliable, but they still had the power and the range to devastate Moscow. And the Russians knew it.

This offer promptly placed Kennedy in a very difficult position as, to anyone outside government circles, it would seem to be a fair and reasonable solution to the problem. For those who were wrestling with the issue, desperately seeking a solution, however, matters were not that simple.

Part of the problem lay in the fact that Turkey had, from the beginning of the crisis, been vehemently opposed to removing the Jupiter missiles. They had only recently been installed and the Turkish government saw them almost as a symbol of national prestige. Kennedy certainly did not wish to lose an ally over out-of-date weapons.

The possibility of a Soviet attack on Turkey was quite real. If this should happen, Turkey, as a member of NATO, could call on powerful allies, including both America and Britain. The prospect of all NATO countries being drawn into the ensuing conflict was a frightening thought.

In his second letter to President Kennedy on 26 October, Khrushchev had likened the dilemma they were in to being bound up by a coil of rope: 'We and you ought not now to pull on the ends of the rope in which you have tied the knot of war because the more the two of us pull the tighter the knot will be tied.'[11]

Far from easing the pressure on the rope, bringing Turkey more fully into the problem simply added another strain on the halter. It was not what Khrushchev intended.

Robert McNamara, along with Sorensen and Bobby Kennedy, was probably JFK's most significant advisor during the crisis.

The Soviet premier wanted a way out that would leave the Soviet Union with at least some dignity. It was an admirable stance, but to many it seemed that all he had done was cause more confusion.

And so the debate raged, with members of EXCOMM and the Presidium meeting for most of the day. Nobody on either side had yet come up with a solution that would please all parties and sometimes, as desperation and doubt increased, it seemed as if they never would.

Meanwhile, the Soviet transport vessels were inching closer and closer to the quarantine line. No Russian ship had yet been stopped and searched, the confrontation everyone dreaded. But the longer discussion went on, the further away a solution seemed. The hands of the metaphorical Doomsday Clock crept closer and closer to the midnight hour.

8. BLACK SATURDAY

Bobby Kennedy later said that Saturday, 27 October was perhaps the most stressful and dangerous day in the whole crisis. To the Americans it was 'Black Saturday', when things could so easily have got out of hand. It was the time when, more than any other moment during that tense and terrifying fortnight, the world tottered, slipped and began to roll ever closer to the chasm that represented the beginning of the Third World War.

Kennedy had expected the Soviet Union to counter the blockade around Cuba by building up more and more pressure on West Berlin. It did not happen. It would be wrong to say that Khrushchev had lost stomach for the fight; he was, after all, the man who had begun the whole sorry episode. But he was someone with surprising insights and, at heart, he was a man with understanding and humanity, and not always the tub-thumping bully that everyone thought they saw.

Bobby Kennedy addresses a rally.

The missiles on Cuba were part of his policy of brinkmanship. As he repeatedly claimed in later days, they were never intended to fire, but simply to threaten and terrify the Americans into leaving Cuba alone. There were, as yet, only a limited number of warheads for the missiles. Now, after several days of worry and concern, of bluff and counter-bluff, the crisis had deepened as his policy of brinkmanship had begun to unravel.

Khrushchev envisaged the whole world exploding into nuclear war. It was a terrifying image for the Soviet premier. If he could avoid it happening, even at the expense of his own position and career, it was something he felt he had to do. Hence the introduction of a new bargaining tool, the US missiles in Turkey.

The increased threat to world peace had begun during the night of the 26th/27th when Soviet battlefield missiles moved into positions where they could launch an assault on the US naval station at Guantanamo Bay. Their new positions were just 15 miles from the American base and had been pre-prepared. All the Soviet soldiers had to do was wait for the order to fire, and remain hidden from the cameras of the US spy planes.

The danger level went up another notch when US listeners realized that Cuban call signs over the radio relating to the air defence of the island had been replaced by Russian ones. No longer was Spanish the chatter over the airwaves, now it was Russian. Clearly the Soviets had taken over aerial defence and the implication was that American aircraft flying on missions over the island would be fired on.

A ground-to-air missile, of the type that shot down Rudy Anderson's U-2.

The Cuba–Turkey debate occupied most of the early part of the EXCOMM meeting that Saturday morning. Khrushchev's suggestion offered both sides a way out. After mulling it over, Kennedy decided he was not opposed to this trade-off. Despite the protests of the Turkish government, Kennedy believed that the US Polaris submarines in the Mediterranean could offer far greater protection to Turkey than out-of-date Jupiters.

The Russian offer, however, was at odds with what was actually happening on Cuba. That morning Robert McNamara had arrived in the meeting to report that, far from slowing down or even stopping, work on the Cuban missile sites had intensified, with engineers toiling day and night to get them completed.[1]

It was something that Kennedy and his advisors found difficult to understand, and was certainly not compatible with the messages currently coming out of Moscow. Once again, the Joint Chiefs of Staff fell back on their old position: an air strike that could be arranged for two days' time, if the president gave his approval. The air strike would be followed by a full-scale invasion and, just in case, US forces were alerted that they could be attacking Cuba the following week.

The debate continued until mid-afternoon when a message was received that stopped everyone in their tracks. Kennedy was out of the room, taking a break by swimming in the White House pool. Swimming was both a relaxant and a balm to his aching body, but when he returned he was met with news of a tragic event, something that almost upset everybody's ambitions and hopes for a peaceful end to the crisis. A U-2 aircraft, he was informed, had been shot down over Cuba.

It was something Kennedy had been dreading for days. Piloted by Major Rudolf 'Rudy' Anderson Jr, the downed U-2 normally operated out of Laughlin in Texas, but that morning Anderson and his aircraft were flying from a forward airfield, McCoy Air Force Base, in Florida.

Anderson, a native of Greenville, South Carolina, had made more reconnaissance flights over Cuba than any other U-2 pilot. Like his comrade, Richard Heyser, he was an experienced and capable flyer. A day or so before Anderson's final operation, launched surface-to-air missiles had been spotted close to a US high-level reconnaissance aircraft. From this, and the Russian takeover

Rudy Anderson, the only US casualty from enemy fire during the crisis.

Llewellyn 'Tommy' Thompson, a voice of sanity on Black Saturday.

of anti-aircraft duties, it was clear that defences had been stepped up several degrees. Even so, everyone, from politicians and journalists to the military planners and strategists, was appalled at the news of that Saturday's disaster.

As Anderson's plane approached the Cuban coastline early on the morning of 27 October, two SA-2 SAM missiles had been fired at him. One of them exploded close behind the aircraft, shrapnel slicing into the cockpit and piercing Anderson's pressure suit. He was, experts later said, probably killed at that point. The U-2 broke apart and fell 60,000ft into Cuban territory, Anderson's body still in the shattered remains of the cockpit. The tail section of the aircraft glided on and came down in the sea.[2]

Who ordered the firing of the SAM was, at that time, unknown. Khrushchev told his son Sergei that it was a local Cuban commander but, even then, that was felt to be highly unlikely. The Russians had taken control of the anti-aircraft missile defence of the island. It was later acknowledged that the SAMs had been fired on the orders of Soviet officers Lieutenant General Stepan Grechko and Major General Leonid Garbuz, afraid that the U-2 would spot the newly placed tactical missiles and expose the threat to Guantanamo Bay.

The Russians were acting on their own initiative, against the directives of Khrushchev. Believing that the Americans would see any attack on their planes as a warlike gesture, he had sent orders to the Soviet Commander-in-Chief in Cuba, General Issa Pliyev, forbidding any of the SAM batteries to fire on American aircraft flying over the island. Whatever reason for launching the SAMs, the action tightened the noose around the necks of both the US and the USSR.

The knee-jerk reaction from EXCOMM members was that the US had to attack the SAM sites the very next day. That was what Kennedy had promised would happen should any US aircraft be shot down. The Chiefs of Staff were now intent on holding him to his promise.[3]

Kennedy prevaricated, pushing away the clamouring military hierarchy. Understanding the seriousness of such a move, he told everyone that he wanted to consider his options and fully investigate the crash to decide if it really was a result of missile fire.

There were also now greater ramifications to consider, including the stance of NATO, which up until now, had supported the USA. But how long would that last in the event of an American attack on the SAM sites? Also, with Turkey assuming greater significance in Russian minds, it would be logical to expect the Soviets to retaliate by attacking their neighbour.

The debate ran on and on, everyone trying to get his point of view across. According to Bobby Kennedy, the president was the calmest man in the room, but even he was beginning to run out of patience and the will to continue the discussions.

Eventually, a draft letter from the State Department was presented for the president's approval. The communication was blunt and to the point: the missiles could not be removed from Turkey and therefore no trade-off could take place. Once again, debate raged. Finally, Llewellyn Thompson, former ambassador to Moscow and now one of the junior members of EXCOMM, managed to persuade Kennedy that his best option was to respond only to Khrushchev's original letter, which made no mention of Turkey or the missiles placed there. He could pretend that the second letter had never been received.

The recently released Kennedy tapes make it clear that 'Tommy' Thompson had faith in Khrushchev and a degree of admiration for the Soviet stance. He believed that there

Soviet Foreign Minister Andrei Gromyko and the Soviet ambassador the the US, Anatoly Dobrynin, meet with President Kennedy, 18 March 1962. Gromyko assured JFK that the Cuban missiles were purely defensive.

was still a chance of the Soviet premier backing down. In response to Kennedy's growing despondency and belief that they were at stalemate, Thompson responded: 'I think there's still a chance we can get this line going … The important thing for Khrushchev, it seems to me, is to be able to say, "I saved Cuba; I stopped an invasion."'[4]

Kennedy agreed. He instructed his brother Bobby and Ted Sorensen to retire to another room to draft an alternative response. He would then look at the two proposals and make a decision about which one to send.

Sorensen was, among other things, Kennedy's speech writer. He was the man who had penned the immortal lines for the president's inaugural address, 'Ask not what your country can do for you – ask what you can do for your country'. A bright and capable advisor to the president, he was someone whose opinion JFK valued most highly. Along with his brother and Robert McNamara, Sorensen was clearly a part of the president's 'inner circle' and deeply involved with presidential decisions during the missile crisis.

It took Sorensen and Bobby Kennedy only three-quarters of an hour to draft an alternative reply, which they then brought back into the full meeting. The reply accepted the offer made by Premier Khrushchev in his first letter of 26 October: the Soviet Union would remove the missiles from Cuba, the US would lift the quarantine measures and give clear assurances that Cuba would not be invaded by US forces. There was no mention of the Jupiter missiles in Turkey, but the message was crystal clear. Putting themselves in Kennedy's shoes, Sorensen and Bobby Kennedy had written:

> The first ingredient, let me emphasize, is the cessation of work on missile sites in Cuba and measures to render such weapons inoperable … The continuation of this threat, or a prolonging of this discussion concerning Cuba by linking these problems to the broader questions of European and world security, would lead to an intensification of the Cuban crisis and a grave risk to the peace of the world.[5]

It was not without a degree of trepidation that President Kennedy eventually agreed with this alternative proposal. It was, as everyone understood, based on Khrushchev's first offer. Kennedy wondered if the Russian premier, in light of his later insistence on removing the missiles in Turkey, would reject this new olive branch. He was, however, willing to take a chance. He made a few alterations to the text, and then passed it for typing and transmission to the Kremlin.

Secretary of State Dean Rusk now proposed a possible answer to the problem of the missiles in Turkey. The weapons, Rusk said, should not be formally included or referred to in any public statement. The US should let Khrushchev know that, if everything else was agreed, they would happily remove them in the days after the Soviet withdrawal, but only if this part of the agreement remained secret. Kennedy agreed. He had already been considering removing the Turkey Jupiters, along with those in Italy, before the crisis erupted, so now he added a codicil, explaining the offer, in his latest letter to Premier Khrushchev.

Preparations for a sudden offensive by US forces continued, with smart money being on an attack early the following week. When Bobby Kennedy met with Soviet Ambassador

Anatoly Dobrynin on Saturday night, he was charged with making him understand that, if the Russians did not take the missiles out of Cuba, then the USA would.

Acting on Dean Rusk's suggestion, Bobby Kennedy told Dobrynin that removal of the Turkey missiles was a separate problem. The US could not be seen to barter over this. Provided the agreement remained private, the US government would withdraw them within six months.

Officially, the country's attorney general, Bobby Kennedy, was also the president's sounding board, a man who was often looked to for advice in crucial moments. In *Thirteen Days*, Bobby Kennedy wrote perhaps the most perceptive and tragic comment, not just on the crisis, but on the lives of himself and his elder brother. While the letter to Khrushchev was being transmitted, he and JFK sat in the Oval Office and the president talked: 'He talked about Major Anderson and how it is always the best who die. The politicians and officials sit at home pontificating about great principles and issues, make the decisions, and dine with their wives and families, while the brave and the young die.'[6]

Bobby Kennedy could not have known it, but within ten years both he and his brother would also die, at the hands of violent and deranged assassins. It makes his words so much more poignant.

There had been another tragedy earlier that day, but the atmosphere in the White House was so tense that nobody really seemed to notice. The shooting down of Anderson's U-2 dominated everyone's thinking, somewhat masking the unpalatable fact that the US had now lost another aircraft. As it was not due to enemy fire, this loss did not seem to hurt quite as much.

At 6.30 am that morning, a Boeing RB-47 reconnaissance plane from Strategic Air Command, piloted by Major William Britton, crashed on take-off from Bermuda. Britton and his crew were part of a flight detailed to search and find the Soviet freighter *Grozny*, which, it was believed, was carrying fuel for the rockets on Cuba and was now approaching the quarantine zone. The aircraft barely managed to struggle into the air before smashing into a cliff at the bottom of the runway, a hazard that it should have easily cleared.

Britton and his crew of three were killed instantly. A later investigation revealed that the RB -7 had been given the wrong water/alcohol fluid in its fuel injectors, a mixture that was intended to give the aircraft extra thrust on take-off. Effectively, the plane simply did not have the power to get off the runway. Five American airmen had now lost their lives during the crisis.

There was worse to come. The four Soviet Foxtrot-class submarines were now close to the quarantine zone or, in the case of two of them, already inside it. The submarines were being tracked by hunter-killer groups of warships, usually consisting of an aircraft carrier and six or seven destroyers. Each carrier was equipped with anti-submarine helicopters and aircraft.

The submarines had to surface at least once a day to recharge their batteries, when they became more vulnerable to the hunters. Once submerged, keeping track of them was a much more difficult matter. It was also during these dangerous moments on the surface that the Soviet sailors communicated with Moscow.

Foxtrot-class submarine *B59* on the surface, a US sub-hunting helicopter from the carrier USS *Randolph* hovering above.

By the early evening of 27 October, the submarine *B-59*, under the command of Valentin Savitsky, was approximately 100 miles south of Bermuda on the northern edge of the exclusion zone. She had been harassed by aircraft from the carrier USS *Randolph* for the past two days, and had therefore been unable to surface, either to recharge batteries or to make contact with home.

The *B-59* was in a bad way. Her batteries were low, the ventilation system out of action and the levels of carbon dioxide inside her cramped metal hull were approaching danger level. Several men had collapsed from exhaustion and the 120° heat.[7]

The previous week, as the crisis deepened, the Pentagon had informed Moscow that any Soviet submarine located by the hunting groups would be called to the surface by the simple act of destroyers or aircraft dropping practice depth charges – effectively hand grenades – on the vessel. The charges were not intended to damage the submarines, but simply draw them to the surface where their crews could be questioned. It was a ludicrous tactic, but to make things even worse, this news had not been passed on to the Soviet captains who had no idea whether they were being signalled or attacked.

With the situation on board now desperate, on 27 October, *B-59* took a chance and surfaced. When she was spotted by a Grumman S2-F Tracker from the carrier USS *Randolph*, Commander Savitsky ordered an immediate crash dive. The destroyer USS *Beale* dropped five practice charges, but received no response. The exercise was repeated. Again, there was no response.

The USS *Randolph*.

Savitsky was convinced that his submarine was being depth-charged. Not having been able to contact Moscow for several days, for all he knew war could have broken out between the USA and the USSR.

Once again the world hovered on the edge of destruction. Unknown to the Americans, the *B-59*, like the other Foxtrot submarines was, in addition to conventional weapons, also carrying nuclear-tipped torpedoes. Orders from Moscow had instructed the Soviet commanders that, if their vessels were in danger of being damaged, either by depth charges or by gunfire, they were to fire the nuclear-tipped torpedoes.

The decision to fire the torpedo was to be verified by all three senior officers on board the submarine. That was the failsafe. If any one of them disagreed, then the weapon could not be used. Present on *B-59* was the flotilla commander of the Soviet submarines, Vasily Arkhipov. Like Savitsky, he was an experienced submariner and a man who held the rank of commander. As such, he was one of the senior men on board.

Commander Savitsky, exhausted after weeks at sea and infuriated by the presence of American vessels in the area, decided to use the nuclear torpedo and sent orders for it to be armed. The three senior officers – Savitsky, political officer Ivan Semonovich and Arkhipov – discussed firing the weapon, but Arkhipov vetoed the idea. It was a monumental decision. Lunching the torpedo would have brought death and destruction to the men on the submarine, the American sailors on whichever ship was targeted, and quite probably to the rest of the world.

Vasily Arkhipov has been credited as the man who prevented the Third World War. There is an element of truth in the statement. His understanding of the situation, and the likely consequences of firing the nuclear torpedo, in contrast to a stressed and exhausted Commander Savitsky, put a definite check on a situation that was spiralling out of control as that Doomsday Clock ticked ever closer to the midnight deadline.

Savitsky had few options left open to him. With the need to escape what was rapidly becoming an iron coffin now imperative, *B-59* surfaced in the middle of the American hunters. The sea around the submarine was illuminated, with aircraft continually buzzing the Soviet vessel. In the only act of defiance still available to him, Savitsky ordered that the red flag of the Soviet Union, complete with hammer and sickle, be run up on top of the conning tower.

Over the next few hours, the Americans attempted to communicate with their Russian counterparts, trying to identify which particular submarine they had brought to the surface, but with no success. Even the efforts of Russian-speaking sailors from the *Randolph* failed to elicit any favourable response.

In an act of universal suffrage, typical of men in difficult wartime conditions when they came face to face with their opponents, some American sailors tried throwing chocolate and cans of Coca-Cola to the submarine. It was done in friendship and generosity, but unfortunately the chocolate and Coca-Cola fell short and ended up in the sea.

After ordering his men to show only 'the stone face' of Soviet resolve to the imperialist Yankee sailors, Savitsky decided to remain on the surface until his batteries were fully recharged, even though he was surrounded by the American destroyers. It took two whole days. Then Savitsky submerged, reversed course and managed to escape.

Knowing there was no chance of getting inside the quarantine zone, let alone reaching his supposed destination, the Russian commander reluctantly headed for home.

One other Foxtrot also suffered the agony and embarrassment of being forced to the surface by the Americans. Additionally, the luckless *B-130*, which had suffered from technical problems throughout the voyage, had to be towed back to Russia after its engines broke down. Only one of the Russian submarines reached Cuba and so fulfilled its mission.

The Foxtrot flotilla returned to Murmansk where their captains received a very unfriendly, even openly hostile, welcome from the authorities. The fact that the submarines were outdated and in a bad state of repair was conveniently forgotten.

It could have been so much worse. As the last event of a thoroughly depressing and dangerous day, the submarines and their fates, *B-59* in particular, could have easily triggered the start of the Third World War.

9. PEOPLE AND PROTEST

The Cuban Missile Crisis happened over fifty years ago, but there are still men and women who remember the excitement and the fear that it engendered.

In America, most citizens knew nothing of the missiles on Cuba until President Kennedy spoke to the nation on that Monday, 22 October. The decision to keep the news secret was, overall, a sound one. It gave the president and his advisors time and space to make crucial decisions, without the pressure of the public and the press constantly bombarding them with queries and concerns.

The president's broadcast was, however, a serious jolt for most of the country. Nobody had quite realized how serious the situation had become. They did now.

Gary Simson (Haines City, Florida):

I had just graduated from High School in Ohio and it came as a shock to me – and to all my friends. We knew there was animosity and tension but none of us suspected nuclear weapons. After that broadcast I did think – we all thought – that war was a real possibility. Whether it would be against Cuba or the Soviet Union I didn't know. And none of us knew if it was going to be a nuclear war or just a conventional encounter.

Russ Shawe (Delaware):

I was twelve years old at the time, living in Delaware. I remember hearing that the situation was bad and that there could be war. I distinctly remember thinking 'I'd better go outside and ride my bike – could be the last chance I ever get.' It didn't happen and I rode that bike for the next couple of years.

Deborah Burmeister Leibecki (Jacksonville, Florida), from *The Florida Times-Union*:

We were given metal bracelets that had our full name, address, religious faith, phone number and mother's name on it. I still have mine after all these years.

Joyce de Forrest (New Jersey):

We all thought that this was the beginning of the build-up to a nuclear war. When you listened to Kennedy it was obvious that we were going to do something. As for what happened over the next few days, most of us were in the dark. I think I learned more about the Cuban Missile Crisis after it was all over than I did at the time.

Ernest Weiskugl (Chicago):

> I lived through the crisis so I suppose I should know lots about it. But at the time you
> were frightened and that just took over. So I wasn't really aware of what was happening.
> I guess I learned most of what I know now from History lessons in school, after it was
> all over. They taught you modern History in those days. That and Geography lessons –
> where I learned all about Cuba – they taught me far more than the newspapers and TV
> at the time.

The idea of 'being kept in the dark' was something that many Americans felt, possibly as
a result of the secrecy that had cloaked the early build-up. Television and newspapers had
remained stubbornly silent. Even after Kennedy made everything public, there were still
some events about which the public knew next to nothing.

There was little grievance at the government decision to keep matters quiet. Most
Americans were either too shocked or too frightened to do more than agree with the
way Kennedy and his advisors were handling the situation. For men in the military, they
knew they had a job to do, a duty to perform. While there was fear – inevitably of the
unknown – there was also confidence and bravado.

President Kennedy visits the Naval Air Station at Key West, 26 November 1962.

Al Scalise (Orlando, Florida):

I was brought up in New York. My mom was from Sicily but I was raised in what they called Little Italy in the Big Apple. In 1959, I joined the US Marine Corps and spent the next few years training on one base or another.

Now I believe in whatever is good for the USA and when we were told about the Soviet missiles on Cuba I knew we had to do something. Those missiles were too close to us, they were dangerous. In the Marine Corps you learned to take orders, not question them. So, if we'd been told 'You're going in' we'd have done it, no problem. I'd been combat trained, schooled in using all the weapons, I was ready. We were all of us ready to invade Cuba. We didn't know what was facing us but that didn't matter. We were ready to go. But, of course, it never happened. I like people who talk straight, who tell it like it is. That's what Kennedy did during the Missile Crisis. He sorted it out so we didn't have to.

Chuck Leadbelly (California):

I was in the Air Force at the time of the missile crisis, posted to an air base near Albuquerque. I wasn't a flyer; I was involved mainly with supplies and administration. There was a lot of talk about war but we weren't frightened. We were well trained and we were ready. Kennedy had to do something about those Russian missiles and he called Khrushchev's bluff. It worked and we didn't go to war. But, you know, if we had been sent in we'd have won easily. We'd have beaten anyone, any country, at that time. We had the strongest Air Force, the strongest Navy and the strongest Army in the world. We were ready and willing, on alert to go in. But the call never came.

Howard S. Palmer (Mandarin), from *The Florida Times-Union*:

I was in the Navy, stationed at NAS Jacksonville in a photo reconnaissance squadron ... The Duty Officer came tearing into the office demanding to know if I could work on the Crusader camera gear. I told him I could and so I saw the Russian missiles on the ground in Cuba.

The corporate military mind was geared for combat. If the troops were not exactly eager to attack, they were certainly not opposed to it. There still remains, in many American servicemen from the time, almost a sense of regret that they were not sent into action.

Overconfidence it may have been, but the sense of regret and missed opportunity remains strong at many levels. The day after an agreement was reached, even though it was all over and the missiles were about to be removed, one senior military advisor still advocated a strike against the Russians. No wonder Kennedy was afraid of his Joint Chiefs of Staff.

Although troop preparations were camouflaged under the scarcely believable blanket of a 'military exercise' that fooled neither Cubans nor Americans, they caused confusion and uncertainty in the country, particularly in those areas, like Florida, which were dangerously close to Cuba.

Van de Mark (Orlando, Florida):

It was a terrifying time. There were troop convoys rattling and sweeping through town, aircraft screaming overhead, low and threatening. I guess it was a bit like the build-up of troops going into Normandy in 1944, trucks and tanks and soldiers everywhere. We were all expecting a war but, thank goodness, Kennedy and Khrushchev saw sense and stopped it.

Jorge Brunet-Garcia (Jacksonville, Florida), from *The Florida Times-Union*:

My family emigrated from Cuba in 1960 after Fidel Castro nationalized most businesses ... We were living in Miami Beach and I remember the 'duck and cover' drills at school. We knew Miami would be one of the first targets if there were hostilities. There was nowhere to hide, nowhere to go.

Not everyone was unduly concerned. Children continued playing, many of them blithely unaware of the looming disaster. Many adults were content to just shrug and leave it all to fate and the politicians.

David Charles 'Tommy' Cohen (Jacksonville, Florida):

In the autumn of 1962, I had just graduated and was living in the Cape Canaveral area. I can't say I was unduly worried at the prospect of nuclear war – one bomb would end it all, anyway. Better to die quickly, I thought, than to survive. There wouldn't have been much to survive for.

Jeff Bellantuone (Connecticut):

I don't remember much about the crisis – I was just a kid, more interested in riding my bike and climbing trees. My dad was a cigar smoker – like I am now – and before it all began you could get good quality Cuban cigars quite easily. Not once Kennedy put on his embargo. The only place you could get them was through Ireland, would you believe. They must have had some sort of agreement with Cuba.

Embargoing cigars or not, as far as the American nation was concerned, the hero of the hour was John F. Kennedy. They regarded him as the man who stood up to the underhand tactics of the Soviet Union, beating Khrushchev at his own game: brinkmanship. It was a simplistic view that took no account of the attitude and thinking of the Russian premier. But there is no denying that the emotion was both real and genuine.

Van de Mark (Orlando, Florida):

When Kennedy addressed the nation that first Monday night my view was that he'd got it just about right. He was dynamic and charismatic, very powerful. He came across, I thought, as being quite brilliant, the ideal man to handle the country in this time of crisis.

Jeff Bellantuone (Connecticut):

> Kennedy was a hero in our house. After the crisis my mom put a picture of him up in the dining room. And we weren't the only ones, either. When he got shot it was dreadful. We were all sent home from school; people were crying and there was a real sense of loss. The closest thing I ever saw to that emotion, that grief, was when Princess Diana died. There was a sense of national mourning. Mass hysteria I suppose but that's what it's like when you lose a hero.

A sense of 'controlled panic' descended over much of the USA. Marine recruiters in New York were amazed, on the day after Kennedy's announcement, to find a line of would-be enlistees stretching right around the block, all eager to serve.

Many people, particularly in the most threatened areas along the eastern coast, immediately began to build themselves fallout shelters.

Ed Haka (St Mary's, Florida), from *The Florida Times-Union*:

> My father and brother took out some of the blocks that made up a wall in our cellar and dug a small room, approximately 6 feet wide, 10 feet long and 5 feet high ... if a nuclear attack occurred we would move to the 'shelter' and live there for at least two weeks waiting for the fallout to disperse.

David Charles 'Tommy' Cohen (Jacksonville, Florida):

> As a Jew, my Dad had been in hiding in occupied Holland right the way through the Second World War so he knew fear. By 1962, he was living in Jacksonville in northern Florida and realized that with three naval bases in the town it was a prime target. He decided to build a refuge.
>
> So he turned his hallway into a shelter. It was only a small space with five doors leading off it into bedrooms, bathroom and the living room. What he did was to line all the walls, the ceiling and the doors with lead. You can imagine how heavy those doors were, covered by sheets of lead. I don't know how effective all that lead would have been. Luckily we didn't have to find out. But the lead-lined hallway was still there when we sold the house some years later.

Lauren Brown (Bristol, Virginia):

> I was living in Washington DC, a very visible place to be with all the TV news coverage, and Ground Force Zero for a psychological strike. My dad was in the USAF at Andrews Air Base and we were living in an off-base rented house. It was a strange time with air raid drills in school, having to hide in the school basement with a mess of tinned food all around. Remember, this was the era when people were told to hold a newspaper over their heads if they were caught outside in a nuclear attack! Newspaper – really?

I was 13 years old in October 1962 and my mum got this weird idea to build a 'safe room' – a makeshift fallout shelter – in our basement. Living in DC we would have been annihilated and my dad knew that. He also knew that I knew. So did my brother. But mum? I think my mother was living in cloud cuckoo land.

The shelters varied in size and strength according to the space available and the ability to create something at least relatively viable in the time allowed.

Lauren Brown (Bristol, Virginia):

Our shelter was pretty shocking. Dad made the walls from our metal bi-fold closet doors. We had no doors on our closets for two years after that. The basement was big, large enough to roller skate in – until 25% of it got made into a shelter. It was pretty makeshift. The walls were the closet doors and they enclosed an area with the laundry tub and hot water heater. I don't know what we were supposed to do with our poo and wee. I can't remember. Perhaps I just don't want to remember.

For many Americans, the end of the crisis did not spell the end of worry and concern. Disaster had been avoided this time, but the future was an unknown quantity where anything might happen if the politicians and leaders got it wrong.

Van de Mark (Orlando, Florida):

It was just as scary after missiles were pulled out, perhaps more. Nobody knew if it would all blow up again. Castro was such an unpredictable man, you just couldn't read him. And then, of course, the Russians went into space in a big way. We didn't know what they could be firing at us from up there. Your imagination just ran riot. So, the Missile Crisis was over – but it wasn't over, if you see what I mean.

David Charles 'Tommy' Cohen (Jacksonville, Florida):

Having been through the recent war my Dad knew that the key to survival was to be prepared. So he began stockpiling goods, things that he would be able to trade. We didn't know it at the time but he had 30 or 40 big tins of Crisco, vegetable oil used for baking. And toothpaste, he had loads of that – all part of being prepared.

The Cuban Missile Crisis affected millions of people. The whole world was, for a brief time, balanced on the edge of destruction. For those in Europe, where the media followed the affair in detail, it was possibly even more terrifying than for people in the USA. Even though they could not actually control anything, many Americans felt that they were part of the crisis and that their president was handling things as best he could. So there was concern, but not the terrifying panic that might have been expected. Not so in the rest of the world and, in Britain in particular, there was a considerable degree of fear.

It was part of an emotion controlled by time and distance. Most Britishers could think back to an era when their country was in control of everything, the empire running affairs with the standard response of 'send in a gunboat' whenever there was a crisis. Now, however, in the post-war world of 1962, that control had passed to the USSR and the USA.

Almost bankrupt after the Second World War, Britain had been humiliated by the recent Suez Crisis, and had suffered from a series of localized conflicts where the supposedly once happy nations of the empire were fighting for their freedom. The country was in dire economic straits. While the beginning of the special relationship between the UK and the USA would, in time, give the country a better standing in the world, in 1962 there was a distinct feeling of being washed up as a great nation.

So the British people stood by and watched. The main emotion was helplessness. The world was facing extinction and Britain could do nothing about it. Other people, other nations, were controlling their fate and, as in any situation where people feel helpless and insecure, fear soon took over.

Mike Evans (Cwmbran, Wales):

I was in the first year of my A Levels. I was taking science subjects but once a month we had a Current Affairs lecture. And, of course, in October 1962 we discussed the Cuban Missile Crisis. It was absolutely terrifying for us, young boys – it was an all-boys

An RAF Victor bomber, one of Britain's V-bomber force.

school – at the beginnings of adult life. For weeks afterwards, every time I heard a door bang I thought it was a bomb dropping.

Anne Hughes (Bridgend, Wales):

I was just ten years old and I'd recently come out of hospital. I'd had meningitis and nearly died. Now everybody was talking about dying again. Every night before I got to sleep I used to check under the bed just to make sure Castro or Khrushchev weren't there, waiting to grab me when the light went out. I didn't really know who Castro and Khrushchev were. I'd heard their names on TV and radio and dad and my brother were always talking about them. But I was too young to understand the real significance of what was happening. I just remember the fear.

Clifford James (Blackwood, Wales):

The whole thing gave me nightmares. I was at College, in Halls of Residence in Swansea. I remember dreaming that there was a bright light outside my bedroom window. In the dream I got up and opened the curtains. Over the bay, out at sea, there was this huge mushroom cloud. I remember thinking to myself, there's going to be blast or shock waves any minute now; I've got to get away. I never knew what happened after that because that's when I woke up.

Dave Salter (Cardiff, Wales):

I was just thirteen at the time but I can remember the Cuban Missile Crisis very well indeed. We would sit there, all the family, ears glued to the radio – the wireless as we called it. There were a lot more news programmes on the radio in those days as well as news flashes whenever anything serious happened. Jack de Manio is the man I remember – he seemed to be on all the time – but there were lots of others as well. I remember thinking, 'Oh my God, what's going to happen to us? Will we go to war?' I couldn't help thinking that the end of the world was coming.

The place where you were living invariably had an effect on the way you viewed the crisis. A hill farmer in mid-Wales or a crofter in the Highlands of Scotland would hardly feel the same way about events as someone living in London or near one of the great naval or air bases. The vast, empty spaces of the world certainly seemed a lot safer than the more urban environments.

Carole Ann Smith (Bulawayo, Zimbabwe):

I had just moved to Rhodesia with my parents. My father was an electronic design engineer and he'd been 'head hunted' by a Rhodesian company. I was young, too young to really know what was going on, but I can remember mum and dad listening to the wireless and talking about the crisis. The constant theme, in all their conversations, was, 'Thank goodness we've moved to Africa. Just in time!' It just seemed as if things were blowing up or falling apart in the world. In Rhodesia I felt safe. We were concerned about relatives still living back in the UK, worried about what might happen to them. It was a real fear. Mum's mother actually moved to Africa to be with us; that was in 1962. She made her life out there.

London, perhaps more than anywhere else, was the last place people wanted to be, more dangerous for those brief weeks than either New York or Moscow:

'According to well-placed Soviets, London would have been the first place to face nuclear attack by Russia and her Premier Nikita Khrushchev because London was closer to Moscow than Washington.'[1]

How people reacted when they heard the news about the Cuban missiles varied greatly. Some were blasé, others clearly terrified. And yet work had to go on.

Jackie Phillips (Cardiff, Wales):

When I was in my second year of secondary school (miles from home in boarding school just outside London), I went into my cookery lesson, first period after lunch, to be told by the teacher that the world would end at 3.30 pm. We were all shocked and perplexed rather than worried – after all she was a very odd woman. Instead of doing cookery, which I assume she thought would be a waste of time, we had a theory lesson on vitamins. It wasn't until later that we put two and two together and realized, at tea time, that it was all about the Cuban Missile Crisis – and that it was probably over.

Strange as it seems, there were still people in the country who had little or no recollection of the crisis. For some, realization came suddenly.

Jacqui Evans (Cwmbran, Wales):

I was at St Julian's School in Newport at the time. It was an all-girls school, just a couple of miles from Cwmbran where my future husband Mike was going to school. He knew all about the crisis, him and his mates. Me? I knew nothing. It just passed me by. Not just me, the other girls as well.

Squadron Leader Ken Deveson:

I was still a schoolboy when the crisis blew up. Of course I knew about it and thought everyone else did, too. After school I joined the RAF and flew Vulcans, long after the crisis was over. But I remember one of my flying instructors telling me that in October 1962 he only realized how serious things were when he got immediate clearance while flying over London. He was flying a Hastings, distributing V force ground crew to different dispersal areas and he went right through the Heathrow zone with absolutely no trouble. Civilian traffic was just moved out of his way. He knew, then, that the crisis was pretty serious.

An anonymous subscriber to the *P Prune* website wrote, 'At the time of the Cuban Missile Crisis, I was in my final year at prep school – we weren't told anything.'

For most people, however, the anxiety was endemic, no matter how well prepared or trained you were. It even affected servicemen who had little or no fear for themselves, but could not avoid concern about their families who would be left behind if the V-bombers flew.

Air Vice-Marshal Michael Robinson:

I was Commanding Officer on a Victor bomber squadron at RAF Wittering. One of my memories is of arranging for my wife and two children to see my parents in Putney, London, as had been planned. I had to give her a cover story about why I was not there. She duly repeated it to my father. He just looked at her and did not believe a word.

Wing Commander Peter West:

My wife later remembered what I had said to her – 'If you see us taking off, take our three children, put them in the car, put a few things in with them, and get the hell out of there. The thing is, please survive.

If well-trained and experienced flyers could think like that it is not surprising that young people on the fringe of adulthood found the time trying.

Roger MacCallum (Glynneath, Wales):

I was studying for my A Levels – though studying is probably a misleading word! Friends and I used to talk about the crisis and we all came to the conclusion that we were a prime target. I was living in Pembroke Dock, on Milford Haven, and if I looked out of the window I could see oil refineries all the way down the Haven. The place had recently become the major oil port in Britain and we all knew that if just one bomb was dropped on that lot, it would be the end of everything. One bomb and that would be it.

In America, particularly in the southern states, people prepared for the nuclear holocaust that might come, but they did it in a relatively orderly manner. Things could easily have slipped into an Orson Wells *War of the Worlds*-style chaos – it is a tribute to the public's faith in John F. Kennedy that they did not. Even so, people were ready for the worst.

The highway south of Cape Canaveral was packed with military vehicles and SAM missile sites were being set up everywhere. Most people filled up their cars with gas,

A Valiant bomber landing after a practice flight.

even their cabin cruisers and boats. Just in case. Everyone believed that a giant orange glow would soon appear over Miami or Orlando and then the best thing to do would be to head for the Everglades.[2]

Thanks to the BBC and a regular supply of newspapers, people in Britain were well aware of the crisis and what was happening over in Cuba. What they were not so well informed about was the strength of the British nuclear deterrent and the level of readiness of the RAF. Put simply, the RAF was well prepared. In April 1962, RAF Corporal Doug Gawley commented on the situation: 'We were a little more knowledgeable about what was happening than the general public and our thoughts on the matter were more intense than the less-informed civilians.'

The arming of the RAF's nuclear weapons was stressful. It was what the pilots and air-crews had trained for, but most airmen still regarded the bombs as a deterrent, something that would keep nuclear war at bay simply by the threat of what they could do. So now, to see them on the airfield and being attached to the aircraft, was not a pleasant experience. Inevitably, there was the issue of safety, as indicated by Air Commander Norman Bonnor, at the time with Navigator Radar: 'They were deliberately designed to be extremely safe, but to definitely go off when you wanted them to. They therefore had things hanging out underneath that were screwed in when you went to Readiness State 5.'

Corporal Gawley continues:

The Base went to Alert 2 on Tuesday, 23 October and Alert 3 the next Saturday. My role extended to the safety and loading of nuclear armaments to our aircraft. Our weapons arrived during Wednesday and Thursday and we began loading them immediately onto the aircraft. Each loading took around six hours with 'Live Weapons' at completion ... Each weapon was subject to a 'Fish Fry' inspection, so called because the unit looked like those fryers built out of stainless steel in local chip shops.

Britain's main deterrent was vested in the strength and power of the V-bomber squadrons. Armed with nuclear bombs, in the event of war their targets would have been Russian towns and industrial centres, missile bases and airfields. As the crisis deepened, the V-bombers were placed on higher alert.

Victor co-pilot John Laycock:

At the start of the crisis each V-bomber squadron had one aircraft and crew on QRA [Quick Reaction Alert], at 15 minutes' readiness. On my Squadron this meant being locked in Operations, the Squadron Offices or adjacent overnight accommodation with crew transport immediately available to go if the aircraft readiness state was raised. As the crisis developed, a second, then a third and a fourth aircraft and their crews were brought to 15 minutes' readiness.

Squadron Leader Jack Connelly:

Quick Reaction Alert was when we put on all our flying kit and lived in it. We never took it off from the minute we went into QRA until the minute we left it. We ate in it, slept in it, we did everything in it. It must be remembered that they were rubber suits, so they got quite uncomfortable.

NBS Technician Mick Connock:

I was placed on Starter Crew, where we had four Vulcans on the scramble pad at the end of the runway. The aircraft were loaded with nuclear weapons and we

One of many protests that were organized around the world against American involvement in Cuba. This one took place in Hyde Park, London, in October 1962. (Photo Don O'Brien)

stood there for some time with the aircrew on board. The most harrowing moment was when they got the order to start engines. I remember thinking what do I do if they go?

Connock was referring to occasions when the V-bomber crews were brought up to Readiness State 5, which meant manning the aircraft and being prepared for an immediate scramble. Mostly, however, crews waited alongside their planes.

Wing Commander Peter West:

We lived in a caravan alongside our aircraft and, in spite of it being late autumn, the weather was mild. So we sat outside in deckchairs, chatting, reading newspapers, books, or playing cards or board games. Food was brought to us in hot boxes and there was plenty of tea and coffee.

Our target was somewhere in North West Russia. I can't remember the name but we spent many hours studying it until we were as familiar with it as our home town. That was also true of the approach to the target. And, of course, we knew what to expect from the Soviet defences.

To be on a V-bomber crew was the ultimate ... There was something about it. One of my colleagues described it as being like a marriage without the sex. The five-man crew of a V-bomber felt so close to one another.

It was a tense and troubling time for everyone. MacMillan, as the country's prime minister, had pledged Britain's support, but the mood in the country varied.

Sir Michael Beetham, then group captain at Bomber Command:

MacMillan played down the British involvement in the affair, but what people didn't realize was that we had the entire force of V-bombers standing at 15-minutes readiness, bombs loaded and with the crews kitted up and ready to go, to drop nuclear bombs on Russia. The whole thing seemed unreal. I remember on the Saturday of the critical weekend, when the crisis was at its worst, I went above ground for about ten minutes to get some air, and the whole nation only seemed interested in some bloody football match.

Alan Frank Millership, RAF Police:

I was a 19-year-old corporal in the RAF Police, employed on Quick Reaction Aircraft Security duties. I can honestly say that it was the most thought-provoking time of all my service activities, and that includes the many terrorist zones I served in throughout the world.

Victor co-pilot John Laycock says: 'The mood in the Squadron was one of lots of nervous energy looking for a place to break out. At 15-minutes readiness there is no opportunity to do anything much except be ready to respond immediately to any call.'

All the time the V-bomber crews knew that, should the call come, not all of them would survive their missions. It was not something anybody spoke about, being too close to each other to acknowledge.

They all thought about the Russian retaliation, however, knowing that their airfields would be prime targets for enemy bombers and Russian missiles, as Wing Commander Peter West contends: 'In the highly improbable scenario where we would take off, we knew that if we did get back, there would be nothing to get back to. It was Doomsday, Armageddon.'

For Laycock, it was the uncertainty: 'We were given little intelligence on the actual situation and so we followed the BBC news bulletins with close interest. It was at least 48 hours after the stand-off was resolved that we were told that the crisis was over and resumed normal readiness.'

The Russian people knew far less about the crisis than the British or Americans. It was, perhaps, inevitable in a totalitarian regime, where individual feelings and responses had been abandoned for the good of the whole nation. Sergei Khrushchev later summed it up in this way:

> They [the people] had information on a limited basis, given the centralized control of the media. The information about the American blockade? Well there was information that

Castro with yet more adoring fans, mostly young.

Soviet ships were moving towards Cuba. But there were no apocalyptic pictures or news
in the papers that tomorrow you could get killed.[3]

Purely because of Britain's geographical location, the RAF was at the forefront of the
likely response and everyone in the service knew it. So, too, did the Americans, as Peter
West noticed when he was given a copy of the US Strategic Air Command magazine
Combat Crew and saw that the normally brash and dismissive Americans were well aware
of Britain's involvement. There, on the cover, was a picture of a Vulcan.

Wing Commander Peter West:

Underneath was the title 'Kissing Cousins'. When you looked at the article, the author
said, 'You guys may think that if you ever have to go over the Soviet Union and drop
your bombs, you will be the first. But you will not, because the Royal Air Force Bomber
Command will have been there before you!'

Given the state of readiness within the RAF, there was little of the gung-ho attitude
that many American servicemen felt when the crisis ended, as Dave Beane, AEO, Victor
Squadron, recalls: 'I remember we were all relieved when the diplomatic negotiations
succeeded and we were stood down – stood down from the hot to trot situation.'

John Laycock:

Eventually all our available aircraft and crews were at readiness and the place was sealed
off. That meant all movement on and off the base was severely restricted. I felt relieved
but impressed when President Kennedy's leadership and resolve persuaded Khrushchev
to back down from what we considered to be a serious case of brinkmanship.

Derek Gawley (corporal, electrical fitter in 1962) adds: 'Of course, we were as pleased as
the rest of the world when Russia backed off. During the crisis I guess we were so pumped
up that we took everything in our stride. We were finally stood down from Alert Status
on 5 November.'

John Laycock explains: 'We had felt we were doing exactly what we were required to
do and making a major contribution to keeping the peace. And afterwards, needless to
say all, bar one crew remaining on readiness, the squadron let off steam in the traditional
RAF manner. Job done!'

When it was all over, when the dust had settled over the potential disaster, there were
stories to be told, stories which, in typical RAF fashion, were self-deprecating and with
almost slapstick humour.

Wing Commander Peter West:

One incident which has remained fresh in my memory is that during a quiet spell our
Navigator Radar Op strolled over to our aircraft and, using a china graph pen, scrawled
a CND [Campaign for Nuclear Disarmament] symbol on the side of the bomb. When he

returned, I asked him why he had done such a damn fool thing, to which he replied, 'If we have to drop that bugger, those CND bastards were right. We never did drop the bomb – those CND B's were WRONG.

If West and the other V-bomber crews were sure that their actions were right and that the bomb was, at the end of the day, a deterrent rather than a weapon, there were many who disagreed with them. Unlike Russia, the so-called 'free world' retained the right to disagree with the voice of their government, or, for that matter, other governments as well.

Many protests in the USA were organized by Women Strike for Peace. Founded in 1961, it was part of the movement that campaigned for a ban on nuclear testing and, later, an end to the war in Vietnam. Rallies and demonstrations, 'sit ins' and mass lobbying of politicians, were the general tactics of the group which, Kennedy later admitted, was instrumental in the adoption of the 1963 Limited Test Ban Treaty.

In many parts of Britain, protests and anti-war marches were organized, invariably aimed at America and with the poster and slogan 'Hands Off Cuba' held proudly aloft somewhere in the throng. These were organized by groups such as 'The Committee of 100' or 'CND', and often involved as many as 2,000 people.

Not always, however. At Midhurst Grammar School in Sussex, forty sixth formers went on strike as a protest against the blockade of Cuba. Refusing to attend lessons, they then marched through town before sending a message to Prime Minister Harold MacMillan.

In Swansea, fifty girls from Glanmor Grammar School also boycotted lessons. Irving Fuchs and Arthur Kato had begun a four-day hunger strike, and in Swansea, 1,000 people demonstrated in support of them. Letters of protest were sent to the Russian and US embassies and to the Foreign Office. It was one of the largest demonstrations ever seen in the South Wales town.[4]

Clifford James (Blackwood, Wales):

I was in college during the Cuban Missile Crisis and took part in what became a torch-light demonstration through Swansea – torchlight because, although it started in the afternoon, it went on into the evening.

After the march, we all had to take up pre-ordained positions in the city. Ours was on the corner by the David Evans department store in the middle of Swansea, three of us standing there with our banner 'Hands off Cuba'.

We were stood there for some time. Then this drunk staggered out of a nearby pub. 'Hands off Cuba?' he shouted, 'I'll show you what I think of Cuba.' He snatched the banner and threw it on the ground, then proceeded to jump all over it, snarling and spitting all the time.

Suddenly a policeman appeared. He was about eight feet tall – well, that's what he seemed to us. He looked down at the drunk and our tattered banner and then pointed his finger directly at the man. The drunk squinted up at him. 'Piss off!' said the policeman.

President Kennedy (back to the camera) and some of the EXCOMM take a breather. (White House photo by Cecil Stoughton via John F. Kennedy Library)

And he did, the bloke just went. We hung around for a bit then went back to our Halls of Residence out in Black Pill.

The writer Robert Nisbet was also at university in Swansea during the missile crisis. The protests and marches managed to find their way into one of his poems. Like most other university students, Nisbet was politically aware, but his poem is as much about the double standards of young men at the time, protesting about 'the big boys' trying to get their hands on Cuba and, at the same time, trying to get his hands on the girl of the moment.

The threat of what the crisis might bring hangs like 'the future's murderous mushroom cloud' – his words – over the easy intellectual life of a student:

32 Hours
Bacon, hot coffee, a new October day, and he goes
to the library, writes his essay on John Steinbeck.
His tutor isn't keen on Steinbeck, but he has
much he wants to celebrate, earnestness and maleness
and socialism in a Californian sun. Later, at one,

they gather for lunch in the snack bar in Saint
Helen's Road, stack placards, reach the march's
starting point by two (first march for some of them).
No War Over Cuba, and he cares, they all care, seem
to sense the throb and heave of missiles cruising
continents. And yet the Saturday is warm, it's a
pleasant day. Tea later, a drink, the dance, again
he falls in love or what feels very close to it. In the
dance hall's resin smells and plangent songs, desire.
And then he walks her home, right the way to Killay,
gropes nearer still to understanding these things.
Back in Hall by two, goes restlessly to bed, sleeps
like the Titanic. Up at eight-thirty, washed and ready
for the rustling notes, feeling again some goodness in
his Californian writer's world. Sunday dinner's
formal, he lets that simply happen, in the afternoon
talks to his room-mate (who will one day be ordained).
They talk of records, cycling routes, but his mind
leaves Geraint far adrift, is full with trembling
of her breast's privilege, the louring
of the future's murderous mushroom cloud.[5]

Students and CND activists provided the main thrust of protest. In general, the protests were more about American involvement than Russian, although no one could quite forget the Soviet missiles. The mantra of the day was 'Hands off Cuba'.

In the main, such protests were tolerably peaceful, causing onlookers to shake their heads and mutter about the folly of youths with too much free time on their hands. Protests took place in cities like Manchester, Glasgow and Bristol but, when over a thousand Cambridge undergraduates gathered to listen to a range of different speakers, the meeting ended in chaos with booing, cheering and shouting.

In many towns and cities across Europe, places like The Hague and Stockholm, there was much chanting, much waving of placards and banners, and the feeling that the Ban-the-Bomb marches of recent years, along with fears of Armageddon, had just gone up to a new level.

Sometimes, however, demonstrations took on a more aggressive mode. On 27 October – Black Saturday in America – a large party of demonstrators marched on the US embassy in London.

The demonstrators were met by several contingents of police who were, according to some of those who took part, 'determined to be rough'. Police officers apparently drove a bus into the crowd and then charged, punching and kicking at the protesters.[6]

As early as the evening of 23 October, a crowd of over 2,000 had gathered outside the American embassy in London before marching on to the Russian embassy, half a mile away. In the words of the *Western Mail*: 'A total of 124 people were arrested as a result of last night's disturbances at the American Embassy. The demonstration was against the blockage [sic] of Cuba.'[7]

The paper went on to claim that 40 per cent of those arrested were women. Six of these were charged with assault and one with larceny of a policeman's helmet – a moment of light relief for the worried readers.

Opinion about the way the Kennedy administration was handling the crisis, notably the quarantine of Cuba, found a mixed response. Many people thought Kennedy had got it right while others took the opposite view.

Dick Roberts Thomas (Cyncoed, Wales):

> I thought that Kennedy had got it so wrong and was backing himself into a corner. Lots of my friends thought the same. We would sit and discuss things when we went to the pub in the evenings – not that we knew much, just what we'd picked up from the papers. It was all very civilized, very British. We thought the Americans really had their hands full dealing with this one. I had not long left school and was living in London at the time and there was a fair bit of anti-American feeling around. Mind you, as events proved, Kennedy got it absolutely right.

One protest did take place in Moscow when several hundred demonstrators gathered outside the US embassy. They assembled in an orderly, good-natured fashion. The supposedly 'spontaneous' protest smacked of being officially organized.

There was no criticism of the Soviet Union during the Moscow protest. All the blame was aimed at America. Protesters were bussed in, and the whole thing was conducted in a formal and exemplary manner, the perfect political protest in fact.

The protesters' banners certainly carried officially approved slogans such as 'Shame on the Yankee Aggressors'. Groups of schoolchildren were ferried to the area to add to the sense of a natural, anti-imperialist outrage: 'The protestors disbanded promptly on an order from the police after exactly four hours, and water-spraying trucks immediately cleaned the road in front of the Embassy.'[8]

It would hardly be possible for a non-government protest, if that is what this was, to have taken place in 1960s Russia where the tentacles of the totalitarian regime were inevitably sniffing out dissident bodies. Carefully orchestrated exhibitions taking place on government orders were another matter altogether.

What the missile crisis did was to polarize people and opinions. As one of the most significant moments of the Cold War, matters could easily have got out of hand. Thanks to the diplomatic efforts of both the US and the USSR it did not happen but, inevitably, the tension and the anxiety forced people to the edges of their rational thinking.

Even for many of the Cuban refugees who had fled the island rather than face Castro's extremism, there were mixed emotions. Many of them still had relatives in Cuba, people they could no longer see or meet on a regular basis, or if ever.

Jorge Brunet-Garcia, from *The Florida Times-Union*:

My uncle, Joaquin Orderqui, who was a commander and quartermaster with the Revolutionary Armed Forces, was tasked with the cat and mouse game of moving and hiding missiles on the ground while the US was trying to document their existence with U-2 flights. I only learned that years later.

Very few people were able to shrug their shoulders and adopt a laissez-faire attitude. You were either for or against the events that were happening out in the Caribbean.

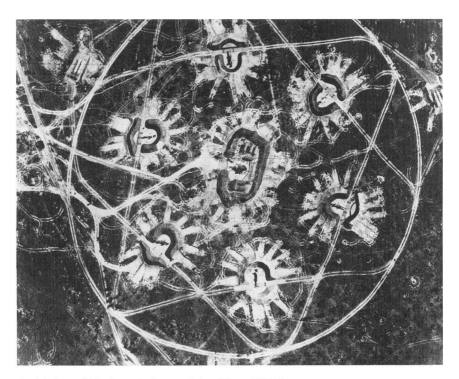

Aerial view of SA-2 launch sites on Cuba. (Photo USAF)

10. AN END TO CRISIS

Saturday, 27 October was a day no one wanted to see repeated. As if crashed aircraft and depth-charged submarines were not enough, on that same Saturday an American U-2 made an accidental, unauthorized flight over the Chukotka Peninsula in the far northwest of Russia.

With its air space violated, the Soviet Union immediately scrambled a squadron of MiGs. The Americans responded with Convair F-102 Delta Dagger fighters and,

Castro cultivating his image – smoking a Havana cigar.

momentarily, high over the Bering Sea, there was the prospect of another confrontation between the two great powers. In the end, both sides recognized the incident for what it was and called their aircraft back to base.[1]

The situation on Cuba remained critical. American reconnaissance flights continued, despite the loss of Anderson's U-2. It was vital that EXCOMM should have up-to-date knowledge of exactly what was happening on the island. On Sunday, 28 October, the CIA was reporting on the latest developments: 'On the basis of aerial photographs obtained from missions flown on Friday and Saturday, we estimate that twenty-four Medium-Range Ballistic missile launchers are now fully operational.'[2]

Whether Kennedy and his advisors slept much after receiving the information is not known. Khrushchev certainly did not, because in the early hours of that Sunday he made a fateful decision.

A few minutes after 10.00 am on Sunday morning, Bobby Kennedy received a telephone message from Secretary of State Dean Rusk. Kennedy had taken his daughters to watch a show-jumping event at the Washington Armory, but what Rusk told the Attorney General now had him gasping in relief. Khrushchev had agreed to withdraw the missiles from Cuba.

The Russian premier had sat for hours contemplating his next move. The fate of the world lay in his hands. President Kennedy had laid out his intentions and clearly showed no sign of backing down. No matter how many times Khrushchev might stress that the missiles on Cuba were there simply to defend the island against attack, the fact that the USSR had initially lied about their presence simply demolished his credibility.

Unlike the missiles in Turkey, which were offering protection to Europe, the presence of nuclear missiles in Cuba could only be seen as part of an aggressive Russian threat to the USA. The fear of a nuclear holocaust haunted Khrushchev. He had begun the scare and now he felt that it was up to him to end it.

Radio Moscow had broadcast the message first, at 9.00 am. In a formal communication to President Kennedy, Khrushchev stated:

> In order to eliminate as rapidly as possible the conflict which endangers the cause of peace, to give assurance to all people who crave peace, and to reassure the American people, all of whom I am certain, also want peace, as do the people of the Soviet Union, the Soviet government, in addition to earlier instructions on the discontinuation of further work on weapons construction sites, has given a new order to dismantle the arms which you described as offensive, and to crate and return them to the Soviet Union.[3]

It was a message that pulled the world away from the brink of war. Khrushchev went on to request one addendum: the US had to remove the Jupiter rockets from Turkey. A refusal on the part of the US would not look good in the eyes of either allies or neutrals. Despite the opposition of his advisors, particularly the Chiefs of Staff, Kennedy felt that removing missiles from Turkey and Italy was, at this stage of the crisis, the least he could do. There was no way that the US could now attack Cuba when Khrushchev's offer would achieve the same effect, without bloodshed.

Kennedy immediately issued a statement commending the Russian premier on his decision to remove the nuclear weapons and agreed to respect the inviolability of Castro's island. Kennedy also pledged not to interfere in Cuba's internal affairs, either directly or indirectly.

The issue of the Jupiter missiles in Turkey was not referred to and was not made public, but as the US had suggested, their removal was assured. Khrushchev accepted this but, with the matter remaining secret, it did look as if the USSR had backed down in the confrontation. It was a message that Khrushchev's rivals in the Kremlin would not forget in the months ahead.

At the White House, the overall feeling was one of joy. In the Pentagon, however, the mood was very different. The Chiefs of Staff were furious.

The events and communications of the previous few days had seemed to lead only into a blind alley. The chiefs felt that Khrushchev would not come to an agreement and even Kennedy had been preparing himself for military action.

Consequently, plans for an air attack and invasion of Cuba had been laid. The assault was to begin on the coming Tuesday, 30 October. Now the chiefs had been forestalled. Curtis LeMay called the agreement 'the greatest defeat in our history', and George Anderson,

A Vulcan bomber with bomb doors open.

who had vacillated between 'hawk' and 'dove', during the whole crisis, announced that this decision would give Castro licence to do as he pleased in the Caribbean and in the Latin-American states.

If Khrushchev had not backed away and agreed to the trade-off of missiles, then an invasion of Cuba would have taken place, to the undoubted satisfaction of the Chiefs of Staff. It would have led to utter chaos: 'Had the Russians used tactical nuclear weapons, whose presence was not suspected by the Americans, a full-scale thermonuclear war would probably have followed.'[4]

Whether or not the Chiefs of Staff would have been so eager to invade had they known about the battlefield missiles remains unclear. Knowing their desire for war against Russia, they probably would have happily launched an invasion, regardless of whatever missiles or weapons were ranged against them. Curtis LeMay was, after all, the man who declared that if there was just one Russian standing at the end of it all, as long as there were two Americans to oppose him then victory would go to the USA!

Castro later said that had the US invaded, he would not have hesitated in ordering the use of tactical nuclear weapons, both from the Cuban artillery weapons and from bombs dropped by Il-28 bombers. Even knowing that it would destroy Cuba would not have deterred him. He was furious when he heard the news that his precious nuclear-armed ballistic missiles were to be removed. He apparently smashed furniture, knocked chunks out of the wall and gave vent to a wide range of curses. Khrushchev had betrayed him, he believed, by reaching a separate agreement with the Americans and not including him in the talks.

Bobby Kennedy, racing back from the horse trials to the White House to share in his brother's moment of triumph, sat and talked to the president for some time:

> As I was leaving he [JFK] said, making reference to Abraham Lincoln, 'This night I should go to the theatre.'
>   I said, 'If you go, I want to go with you.'
>   As I closed the door, he was seated at the desk writing a letter to Mrs Anderson.[5]

The Soviet offer to remove the missiles was not the end of the matter. The US needed to be sure that Khrushchev's words were not simply rhetoric and that the dismantling of the missile sites was actually taking place. So U-2 flights continued, the spy planes soon reporting that the Soviets were indeed dismantling the sites:

> When last covered, Santiago de Cuba Missile Support Facility contained at least 89 missile canisters, 25 probable booster canisters and at least 40 wing or fin crates. San Pedro de Cacocum Support Area contained six canister transporters, at least 100 missile canisters. By [date obliterated], the missile associated equipment, which had been in the open, had been removed except for two canister transporters at Santiago de Cuba.[6]

Castro loved baseball.

The navy continued to enforce the quarantine, even though Khrushchev had now ordered all Soviet ships approaching the blockade line to turn back. Destroyers from the navy had been tracking the Russian tanker *Grozny* for several days. She was now approaching the quarantine area, the first Russian vessel to reach this point. With the news of an agreement not yet passed on to the destroyer crews, there was considerable debate among the commanders about how the ship should be stopped.

At the last moment, the *Grozny* received Khrushchev's order not to breach the blockade line. She immediately stopped dead in the water, before the US ships could do anything.

It was another delicate moment. How the Soviets would have responded – Khrushchev always having called the process of stopping Soviet ships an act of 'piracy' – had the *Grozny* been boarded is yet another debatable matter, but with negotiations at a critical level, nobody wanted to find out. To the relief of both sides, the Russian vessel turned around and headed home.

One factor that clearly emerged from the operations off Cuba was that the US Navy had no idea how to enforce a blockade. A considerable task force, consisting of carriers, heavy cruisers and destroyers had been built up off the Cuban coast, but no thought had been given to the process of stopping ships at sea or alerting submarines to the presence of blockading warships.

Aerial reconnaissance of Cuba also continued for the next few days. Khrushchev had made a point of asking for this violation of Cuban air space to be discontinued, referring in his statement to infringements of Russian territory by spy planes over the past few years. However, Kennedy was insistent that he needed to know how the dismantling of the missile sites was progressing. Using U-2s seemed the only way to adequately obtain this information and, for the time being at least, the flights continued.

He need not have worried, as Khrushchev was as good as his word. Within days, the Soviet missiles, along with their crews, support vehicles and other equipment, were loaded onto eight Russian freighters. Between 5–9 November, the ships began leaving Cuba, and heading back to the USSR.

The Russian soldiers perhaps felt the blow to Soviet prestige more than anyone. They were on the spot, ready to challenge the Americans. Now they were told simply to pack up and go home. To be leaving with their tails between their legs was far from easy. Large numbers of them responded by going to Havana's bars and getting very drunk.

The Cubans, also, were confused and unhappy. It began with their leaders. Che Guevara considered Khrushchev's decision a betrayal of Marxist ideals and of Cuba. Fidel Castro was furious. He immediately put together a five-point document, laying out what he considered essential issues needed for any agreement with the USA. These included an end to the economic blockade of Cuba and an agreement to discuss the thorny issue of the American presence at Guantanamo Bay.

The five points were, really, just an academic exercise, little more than face saving. The Soviet Union and the US had already reached agreement and Castro had little ammunition left.

Ordinary Cuban men and women in the street were also angry. Many of them demonstrated, marching through Havana chanting anti-Russian slogans and targeting Khrushchev for their venom. The cry of 'Nikita, Nikita, what you give you can't take away', supposedly written by Fidel Castro himself, was heard everywhere.

Kennedy had already made an address to the American people, on 2 November, this time with far less foreboding and drama than his original broadcast on 22 October:

> My fellow citizens: I want to take this opportunity to report on the conclusions which this Government has reached on the basis of yesterday's aerial photographs, which will be made available tomorrow, as well as other indications: namely, that the Soviet missile bases in Cuba are being dismantled, their missiles and related equipment are being crated and the fixed installations at these sites are being destroyed.[7]

Kennedy was quick to tell the media that whatever they reported, they were not to crow or gloat. He did not want this to be seen as an American victory, something which just might prompt the Soviets into further action and undo all the good that had so recently taken place.

Even so, it was not long before TV channels and newspapers in Britain, America and the rest of the world were hailing Kennedy as a hero. The general theme or message was that despite the fact that there was no war, Khrushchev had surrendered: 'Kennedy's Cuba Triumph. Mr Khrushchev's announcement of his order to dismantle the bases and ship them [the missiles] back to the Soviet Union was regarded by American officials and diplomats as a remarkable surrender.'[8]

Further negotiations were needed to decide the fate of the Il-28 bombers that had been sent to Cuba. Agreement was soon reached, and the aircraft were duly loaded onto Russian freighters, leaving the island on 5 December.

The USA announced the end of the naval quarantine on 20 November. To everyone's relief, the issue of boarding Soviet ships had never arisen.

By December 1963, it was clear that the USSR had changed both its short- and long-term approach to Cuba. Whilst the missiles had gone, there was still a heavy Soviet presence on the island, but the CIA was happily reporting that: 'Most of the Soviets now in Cuba are advisors and technicians ... There are no organized Soviet ground troops now in Cuba. We estimate the present Soviet strength between 4,000 and 7,000 men.'[9]

The previous twelve months, however, had not been without concerns. Unlike the more destructive nuclear weapons, the Soviet tactical nuclear missiles – or battlefield missiles as they were known – that would have made short work of any invading US troops, were left in place on Cuba.

In a deliberate move, Khrushchev was intent on placating the Cuban leader, who had been left out of the negotiations regarding the long-range ballistic missiles. Castro was feeling decidedly unhappy. His pride had been hurt and there was a possibility that Cuba would sever relations with the USSR. That would not be in the best interests of the Soviet Union which, many Russians felt, had already lost face over the crisis.

It was almost as 'a consolation prize' that the 100 battlefield missiles were offered to Castro. They were not part of the agreement reached by Kennedy and Khrushchev, and as the Americans did not even know of their existence, leaving them on Cuba was not a major problem for the Soviets. Castro, for his part, was happy to see them remain to swell his arsenal.

However, Castro's sudden mood swings and limited ability to think rationally remained frightening. Soviet Deputy Prime Minister Anastas Mikoyan was given the task of going to Cuba and assessing the mental state of the Cuban leader. It was not an easy job, as Castro was unreadable at the best of times. Now his volatility was rampant.

During his time in Havana, Mikoyan saw Castro's emotional difficulties at first hand, his outbursts bordering on paranoia. He was unable to forget that he had been side-lined by the US and USSR. To give such an unstable character control over nuclear missiles, which had an 'explosive force of 100 Hiroshima-sized bombs', would be both irresponsible and self-destructive.[10]

After a four-hour meeting with Castro, Mikoyan managed to convince the Cuban leader that it would be against Soviet law to transfer ownership of the missiles to Cuba. In fact, no such law existed, but this was kept hidden, a wonderful case of subterfuge combined with diplomacy by the Russian politician.

On 22 November, Castro reluctantly acknowledged that the battlefield missiles were going to be withdrawn. They were duly crated and returned to the Soviet Union in December, effectively ending the missile crisis in the Caribbean.

The presence of US missiles in Turkey and Italy had been a contentious issue throughout the thirteen days of the crisis. Kennedy had never been particularly happy with the Jupiter rockets and had considered pulling them out before the crisis began. He had given his word to Khrushchev and, almost as soon as the Soviet weapons were removed, the US began to dismantle and bring home the missiles from Turkey. The last of these was disabled by the end of April 1963, and shipped back to the US shortly afterwards.

And Castro? When he was able to sit back and look at the resolution to the crisis more objectively, he was amazed to see that the affair had caused him no grief or discontent. For the moment at least, his popularity among Cubans on the island remained high.

Overall, the Kennedy–Khrushchev Pact, as it became known, had done him considerably more good than harm. He may have lost his missiles but he had not lost face, which was more than could be said about Khrushchev.

Kennedy's guarantee that he would not invade Cuba, or assist any other nation that was attempting to do so, or was even just considering it, had strengthened Castro's position as Cuban leader. Without fear of attack, he could now concentrate on cementing his position and rebuilding the island's economy.

The first of these was relatively easily achieved. The second was far more difficult, requiring financial and economic aid from the Soviet Union – a temporarily estranged Soviet Union – before it could be even half-way achieved. Castro was clear. He would not break with Russia, he would use the Soviet Union to help shore up the economy of the island.

Soviet missiles in the process of being loaded back onto cargo ships for transport home, Casilda Port, Cuba, 6 November 1962.

11. AFTERWORD

The ramifications and consequences of the Cuban Missile Crisis were considerable. To begin with, it confirmed what everyone already knew, that diplomacy was always more effective than resorting to military action. As Winston Churchill had stated at a White House luncheon in June 1954, 'To jaw-jaw is always better than to war-war.'[1]

In October 1962, there had nearly been 'war-war' and the prospect had frightened everyone. As a result, in 1963 the hot line between Washington and Moscow was set up so that the leaders of the two most powerful nations in the world could actually speak to one another directly before a crisis like Cuba blew up again.

During the crisis, Kennedy and Khrushchev had been reduced to writing letters to each other, a process that often took several hours or even days – hardly the most efficient way to communicate. The hot line would, in future, provide almost instant contact between the two leaders. The hot line, originally known as Washington–Moscow Direct Communication, became in common parlance the 'Red Phone', even though red telephones were never actually used.

In time, the hot-line telephone was replaced by fax and then, since 2008, by a secure computer link. The creation of a direct line between the two leaders was a major step forward. Since its inception, there have been no major confrontations between the two superpowers, certainly nothing to match the Cuban Missile Crisis. Arguments and disagreements, yes, but conflict, no.

Apart from the panic that had seized the world while the crisis was at its height, the public in general reacted in a low-key way once everything was finished and the events consigned to relieved memory.

'Commie bashing' had been something of a craze since the end of the Second World War. This persecution ranged from young boys cat-calling after communist supporters in the streets, to enormous iniquities and miscarriages of justice like the McCarthy witch-hunts. Surprisingly, unlike the mass protests in the early days of the crisis, there was little public reaction once things in Cuba had settled down. Such outpourings of hate require the silence of the imagination to get up a head of steam. It needs, in particular, betrayal by people like the Rosenbergs or Kim Philby, Klaus Fuchs, or Burgess and MacLean.

The Cuban Missile Crisis was too open, too close to disaster for such hate. The communist threat still lingered in people's minds, but after the crisis was over, the American and British public simply said to themselves, 'God bless JFK' and got on with their lives. There was still fear of a nuclear war, but no universal increase in hatred towards the Soviet Union.

In the minds of many, Cuba actually replaced Russia as the bogey-man of world affairs. Hijackers and terrorists might terrify air travellers with their standard line 'Take me to Cuba', but it was a far cry from the threat of a nuclear confrontation between the USA and the USSR.

Castro in pensive mood ... with a glass of wine.

Perhaps the greatest 'loser' in the whole affair was Nikita Khrushchev. He had begun the crisis but, as the world edged closer to catastrophe, he was the man who realized the significance of what was about to happen. He did not want war, shuddering at the prospect of millions of dead Russians and Americans.

President Kennedy did not want war either, but he would have gone down that road if Khrushchev had not agreed to a settlement which, on the face of it, appeared to be a Soviet climb-down. As far as most people were concerned, Khrushchev had agreed to move the missiles out of Cuba in return for Kennedy's agreement not to invade Cuba. And that was all.

By keeping secret the proposed removal of US missiles in Turkey, he effectively sealed his own political fate. To the world it seemed as if Kennedy had won the confrontation between the two leaders. Khrushchev managed to retain control in the Soviet Union for another two years, despite significant criticism from men like Rodion Malinovsky, but in 1964, he lost power when a coup by his former protégée, Leonid Brezhnev, saw him replaced as first secretary. A report of the Communist Party Central Committee made clear the simple fact that Cuba was the cause of his downfall:

Comrade Khrushchev declared that if the USA touched Cuba we would launch a strike against it. He insisted that our missiles be sent to Cuba. This provoked the most serious

Kennedy and Khrushchev pose with their wives for photographers.

crisis, bringing the world to the brink of nuclear war; the organizer of the most dangerous venture himself was greatly alarmed. Having no other way out, we were forced to accept all the demands and conditions dictated by the USA.[2]

A humiliating climb-down was not to be countenanced in 1960s Russia. The agreement to remove the missiles in Turkey was ignored. It had never been made public and so did not count in terms of international standing. The Soviet Union looked inefficient and weak in the eyes of the world, that was all that mattered. Khrushchev's courage and belief in doing the right thing were never mentioned. He had set up a situation that looked as if it would belittle the USA. He failed when Kennedy called his bluff.

Khrushchev must have known the consequences when he pulled the missiles out of Cuba. He had come to prominence during the Stalinist era, a time when political failure meant immediate and harsh consequences. Yet, knowing how his actions would be interpreted he went ahead, not for the good of Nikita Khrushchev or for the Soviet Union, but for the good of mankind.

None of this belittles the courage and skill of John F. Kennedy. He was undoubtedly the champion of the free world and, while there was, inevitably, a degree of luck in the outcome, such perceptive individuals as Robert McNamara remained clear about the president's role: 'For many years I considered the Cuban Missile Crisis to be the best-managed foreign policy crisis of the last century. I still believe that President Kennedy's actions during decisive moments of the crisis helped to prevent a nuclear war.'[3]

The relationship between the Soviet Union and China did not improve in the post-Cuba days. Indeed, the gap between the two most powerful communist nations in the world widened as a result of the missile crisis: 'In the same year [1962] that gap became a gulf as a result of the Cuban Missile Crisis. China fiercely criticized the Soviet Union on two counts: first, for siting its rockets so clumsily that they were easily detected; second, for its craven submission to the American ultimatum'.[4]

The continued antipathy between China and the Soviet Union was yet another factor in Khrushchev's fall from power. He and Mao Zedong had developed a deep dislike of each other. Far from creating the massive communist wall that the West had feared would soon arch its way across Europe, the friction between the two communist countries had split them with a deep and irreversible crevasse.

Speculation can create all sorts of ideas around the motives of China at this time. The Sino-Indian War began on 20 October 1962. It was, of course, at a time when the USA and the USSR were embroiled in events on the other side of the world. Given the poor relationship between the Soviet Union and China, it is hardly likely that this was a coordinated attack. It was more a case of taking advantage of a situation while the world was engaged elsewhere.

The Sino-Indian War lasted barely a month, ending as quickly as it began when Chinese forces were suddenly recalled. It was hardly a major event, but what it did achieve was to heighten the tension and add to the feeling that this was yet another move towards the destruction of the planet.

The number of American fatalities during the crisis varies according to what can be counted as a 'war casualty'. Rudy Anderson was the only American killed by enemy fire, but eleven flyers also died when three Boeing RB-47s crashed before, during and immediately after the crisis. On October 23. a Boeing C-135 Stratolifter delivering ammunition to Guantanamo Bay also crashed, killing seven crew members. Whether these count towards battle casualties depends on the way the events are considered, but they brought the American death toll during the crisis to just over twenty. For the protesters who roamed the streets of London, Washington and elsewhere, it was twenty too many.

Two Russian soldiers were killed during the crisis: Victor Mikheev and Aleksandr Sokolov. They were crushed to death on the night of 26/27 October, when the truck transporting their unit into a position to attack Guantanamo Bay fell into a ravine. Several Soviet soldiers in the truck with them were seriously injured. One unlucky Cuban, who had paused at the roadside to watch the convoy pass by, also died in the accident.

Once the crisis was over and the missiles removed, the status of US forces across the world was returned to DEFCON 4. Shortly afterwards, the body of Major Rudy Anderson was returned to the USA, where he was buried with full military honours in South Carolina. He was awarded, posthumously, the Air Force Cross, becoming one of the first recipients of the new medal.

Anderson's fellow U-2 pilot, Richard Heyser, stayed on in the USAF, retiring as a lieutenant colonel. He died in 2008. Interviewed in 2005, he clearly retained his sense of humour right to the end: no one was more relieved than him that the crisis ended peacefully. He said he did not want to go down in history as the man who started World War Three.[5]

It has been suggested that the success of Kennedy's strategy during the missile crisis was instrumental in America's decision to send increasing numbers of troops into Vietnam. With their role as 'world policemen' reinforced by the successful outcome of the missile crisis, the build-up of US forces in Indochina took a dramatic increase following 1962. If this is true, then the American military planners and leaders did not learn the very simple lesson: diplomacy has always been a better option than military might.

One of the more lasting consequences of the crisis was the horror with which both Kennedy and Khrushchev viewed the preponderance of nuclear weapons in the world. These concerns, a direct result of the Cuban crisis, led to the signing of the first control agreement of nuclear arms in the Cold War period. The Limited Test Ban Treaty was signed by the USA, USSR and Great Britain in 1963. It banned all nuclear testing in the atmosphere, in space and below water. The treaty was not particularly effective in limiting the growth of nuclear weapons, but it did set a precedent for later arms treaties.

Castro, of course, was still in power. He continued to rule despotically, with any opposition contained by his police and security forces. There had always been refugees surreptitiously leaving Cuba, but in 1980, in the wake of a disastrous sugarcane harvest

"LET'S GET A LOCK FOR THIS THING"

An American cartoon captures the post-crisis desire to limit the use of nuclear weapons.

Even after the crisis had ended the US Navy continued to inspect Russian ships as they approached or left Cuba. Here the Soviet freighter *Volgoles* heaves to on 9 November 1962.

and a plummeting economy Castro announced that whoever wanted to leave the island could do so with his blessing. In what became known as the 'Mariel Boatlift', over 120,000 Cubans took him at his word and headed for the USA from the port of Mariel. A similar exodus ten years later led to a further 90,000 leaving the island, many of them on home-made rafts. Castro continued to go his own way, with little or no change to his demeanour.

Khrushchev's 'adventure' in Cuba was, in many ways, a reckless gamble. Had it come off he would have been elevated to a place alongside Lenin and Stalin in the pantheon of heroes of the Soviet Union. His gamble failed and, in Russia at least, he has been virtually forgotten.

The importance of Cuba, and the events of 1962 to the Soviet Union can never be ignored. In the words of Sergei Khrushchev, son of the Soviet premier, America has always been protected by two oceans:

> They're scared of everything as a nation. I would compare America to a tiger that grew up in the zoo and then was sent back to the jungle ... Cuba, after 1961, became for the Soviet Union the same as West Berlin to the United States – a small, useless piece of land deep inside hostile territory. But if you don't defend it you will not be treated as a superpower.[6]

Perhaps that was at the root of Khrushchev's gamble. Outgunned by the quality and quantity of US missiles, it was a desperate attempt at parity. Keeping the USSR in the premier league of nations was never going to be easy, but the green hills and the glorious golden beaches of one tiny island on the fringe of the Caribbean almost helped Khrushchev pull it off.

12. WHERE ARE THEY NOW?

Some of the main players in the crisis, men like the Kennedy brothers and Castro, became household names; others quickly faded from public view. Whether they played a significant role or whether their involvement was peripheral, they all contributed to what was the gravest crisis the modern world has yet seen.

Neither Jack nor Bobby Kennedy managed to live out the 1960s. JFK was famously shot and killed on 22 November 1963, as his motorcade drove along Dealey Plaza in downtown Dallas. In the months following the missile crisis, he had assumed almost mythical status in the USA. It did not stop Lee Harvey Oswald from taking three shots at the president from the sixth floor of the Book Depository building. Two of the fatal shots hit Kennedy in the head and back. He was pronounced dead within the hour.

Bobby Kennedy served for a while as Attorney General in the administration of his brother's successor, Lyndon B. Johnson, before gaining election to the Senate and putting himself forward as a Democrat candidate in the 1968 presidential elections.

Assassination Site President John F. Kennedy

A postcard showing the route of Kennedy's car and the probable location of the sniper on the day of his assassination in Dallas.

Following a massive victory over Eugene McCarthy in the Californian primary on 5 June 1968, he was shot while taking a shortcut through the kitchens of the Ambassador Hotel in Los Angeles. Bobby died the following day. His assassin, a Palestinian named Sirhan Bisham Sirhan, was supposedly unhappy with Kennedy's support for Israel in the recent Six-Day War.

Nikita Khrushchev was ousted from power in October 1964. It was a bloodless coup led by his friend Leonid Brezhnev, but even so, Khrushchev quickly became a 'non-person' in Russian life. When, later, the many-volume work *Great Soviet Encyclopaedia* was published, Khrushchev did not receive a single mention. He declined into a state of almost permanent depression. With security personnel logging his every movement, noting every piece of mail he received, he was virtually a state prisoner during his final years.

Originally told that the house and dacha where he lived would be his for life, he and his wife were later moved to a small apartment. His pension of 500 roubles a month was reduced to 400. He wrote his memoirs, published in 1970, but when he died of a heart attack in September 1971, *Pravda* commemorated his death in just one short sentence.

Not everyone viewed Khrushchev's actions so negatively. The British peer Lord Russell, for one, was clear that the Russian premier had effectively saved the world: 'Mr Khrushchev was personally responsible for the avoidance of nuclear war, Lord Russell said last night: "He has acted with the greatest restraint in a crisis of the first magnitude."'[1]

It was a minority opinion, however, with Russians thinking Khrushchev had failed them, and most people in the West subscribing to the idea of a Kennedy victory.

Fidel Castro died at the age of 90 on Friday, 25 November 2016. Following the Cuban Missile Crisis, he held office and wielded supreme power on the island for over fifty years. As his health declined, he gradually relinquished control to his brother Raúl, before finally stepping down in 2006. Rarely seen in public during his final ten years, Fidel never quite abrogated power completely. Opinions remain mixed about Castro the man and Castro the leader.

On his death, Cuba went into a period of nine days' official mourning. Sporting events and concerts were cancelled, shops and restaurants closed. In Miami, where so many of the exiles – people driven away by the ferocity of Castro's ideas and policies – had settled, it was very different. There was unfettered rejoicing as people took to the streets to celebrate his passing.

His regime was dictatorial and ruthless, marked by lack of tolerance and hundreds of summary executions, of which estimates vary between 200 and 1,500. Castro was unfazed. Not for nothing had he once declared, 'Condemn me. It does not matter, history will absolve me.'

Yet he created social care, medical and educational systems that are still second to none. Later attempts to export his revolution to places like Angola kept his profile at the front of the world's consciousness throughout the 1970s and 1980s.

Castro's real legacy was in the high quality of education he created on Cuba.

Along with Che Guevara, Castro remains, in the eyes of many, the epitome of the revolutionary spirit that gave the 1960s such a veneer and gloss. In the words of Andrew Marr:

> He was, in the true sense, a great poser ... He posed as an ordinary worker in the cane fields; and when he posed alongside Nikita Khrushchev, you could tell that the Soviet leader felt he was in the presence of the nearest thing world communism had to a rock star ... In a hazy and confused way, Castro became the Jimi Hendrix of revolutionary politics.[2]

Ernesto 'Che' Guevara, the Argentinian-born doctor whose name and iconic image became synonymous with the idea of revolution, remains something of a cult figure in Cuba. Posters and sculptures, showing him in his army fatigues and beret, can be found everywhere across the island. It is a little surprising as, unhappy with his role in the government and with the way Castro was ruling, he left Cuba soon after the missile crisis, returning to what he knew best: guerrilla fighting. He was captured by government troops while fighting against the regime in Bolivia and executed on 9 October 1967.

Both Robert McNamara and McGeorge Bundy remained in government until 1968, serving under Lyndon B. Johnson as, respectively, Secretary of Defense and National Security Advisor.

Castro entertaining reporters and supporters in a field outside Havana.

The reputations of both men suffered in later years, as they were instrumental in esca-lating American involvement in the Vietnam War. McNamara, who became president of the World Bank, died in July 2009 at the age of 92. Bundy, the man who first gave President Kennedy news of the Russian missiles on Cuba, died on 16 September 1996.

Ted Sorensen, presidential advisor and speech writer, was devastated by the assassination of JFK. He immediately tried to resign, but was persuaded to stay on to help with the changeover. His resignation was finally accepted in February 1964. He wrote a biography of Kennedy and died in 2010.

The two Americans who had caused Kennedy most concern during the crisis, Admiral George Anderson and General Curtis LeMay, went on to careers of mixed fortunes. The vacillating 'Gorgeous George' Anderson had run foul of McNamara too many times for comfort, both during and after the crisis, and was dismissed as chief of naval operations in August 1963. He had been in charge of the quarantine arrangements, the necessary but badly organized blockade of Cuba. Often, even before the crisis, he was a vocal opponent of Kennedy. He went on to serve three years as US ambassador to Portugal and died in March 1992.

Curtis LeMay, the dogmatic, hard-line commander of the Strategic Air Force, was a veteran of the Second World War, having organized the incendiary bombing raids on Japan. He was the man who had advocated an attack and invasion of Cuba even after the crisis was over, and never moved from his initial stance of military action rather than diplomacy.

In 1968, LeMay ran, unsuccessfully, for the post of vice-president. He continued with his hard-line opinions, being caricatured in the Stanley Kubrick film *Dr Strangelove* as the manic and highly dangerous General Jack Ripper.[3]

Dictator Fulgencio Batista escaped to the Dominican Republic when Castro seized power in 1959, taking with him a fortune in stolen cash. He was eventually granted political asylum in Portugal and died there in 1973.

By the end of 1962, Rodion Malinovsky had become increasingly disenchanted with his friend Khrushchev and with the way the Cuban crisis had been handled. He successfully demanded that the Soviet military be given a greater say in formulating policy, leading, indirectly, to the coup against Premier Khrushchev. Malinovsky died, a celebrated and much-decorated hero, in March 1971.

Oleg Penkovsky, the Russian colonel who spied for MI5 and the CIA, passing on technical information about the R12 and R14 missiles, was arrested on 22 October, the day Kennedy alerted the American people to their danger. He was shot on 16 May 1963, although, for many years, there were rumours that he had been burned alive as a warning to other would-be traitors. In 1966, the CIA sponsored a book about the Russian spy, *The Penkovsky Papers*. It was, in the eyes of many, a dreadful publication, which made a disgruntled, unpredictable and bitter man into something of a saint.[4] It did, however, give him a degree of lasting notoriety.

Victor Arkhipov, the man credited for preventing the Third World War by refusing to sanction the use of a nuclear-tipped torpedo when submarine *B-59* was surrounded by US warships, received little public credit for his actions. At least not immediately. Such recognition as Arkhipov garnered, came much later in his career. He was promoted to rear admiral and, briefly, ran the Kirov Naval Academy. He died in 1998 from the effects of exposure to radiation.

Everyone who was in any way involved with the Cuban Missile Crisis in 1962, was only too well aware that the world had come perilously close to destruction. Whether things were dealt with appropriately, or whether the solution to the crisis was a matter of sheer luck, remains something of a judgement call.

Ironically, the two men who wrestled with the issues and eventually achieved a solution did not live long enough to appreciate the benefits.

President Kennedy's assassination elevated him to an almost mythical position in modern American folk lore. He remains one of the most beloved of all US presidents.

Had he lived, John Fitzgerald Kennedy would undoubtedly have gained a second term at the 1964 presidential elections and gone on to substantial achievements. He might even have back-tracked, as Khrushchev had done, over the missiles, and stopped the escalation of US troops heading for the killing fields of Vietnam.

Nikita Khrushchev, a misunderstood man of courage and humanity, who risked both his political future and his reputation – and arguably even his life – by doing 'the right thing', has been airbrushed out of Russian history, by the Russians at least. Yet this was the man who oversaw the de-Stalinization of the Soviet Union and began the process of giving worldwide credibility to his country.

More importantly, he was the man who, by having the courage to back down from potential disaster, undoubtedly saved the world from destruction. Khrushchev did not always get it right, but with things like the 1962 Cuban Missile Crisis, he was not afraid to admit his mistakes.

NOTES

Chapter 1

1. *Western Mail*, 6 October 1962.
2. Alexander McCall Smith, *Emma*, The Borough Press, London, 2015, page 1.

Chapter 2

1. Ann-Marie Holmes, 'The United States and Cuba, 1898–1953', unpublished MA thesis in Diplomacy and Military Studies, October 2009, page 36.
2. Esther Selsden, *The Life and Times of Fidel Castro*, Parragon, London, 1994, page 2.
3. Ibid, pages 53–54.
4. www.wikipedia.org Cuban Missile Crisis.
5. Michael Dobbs, *One Minute to Midnight*, Arrow Books, London, 2009, page 7.
6. Selsden, page 61.
7. Juanita Castro, My Brother is a Tyrant', *Life* magazine, 28 August 1964.
8. Wikipedia, ibid.
9. Robert Dalleck, *John F. Kennedy: An Unfinished Life*, Allen Laine, London, 2003, page 538.
10. Ibid, pages 536–537.
11. Ibid, page 543.
12. Richard E. Neustadt and Graham T. Allison, 'Afterword', published in *Thirteen Days*, Robert F. Kennedy, W.W. Norton & Co, New York & London, 1971, page 112.

Chapter 3

1. Michael Lynch, *Stalin and Khrushchev: The USSR 1924–1964*, Hodder & Stoughton, London, 2001, pages 110–111.
2. Wikipedia, ibid.
3. Quoted in *John F. Kennedy: An Unfinished Life*, Robert Dalleck, page 535.
4. Robert F. Kennedy, *Thirteen Days*, W.W. Norton & Co, London, 1971, page 28.
5. Michael Dobbs, page 43.
6. Arthur Schlesinger, 'Foreword' to *Thirteen Days*, page 10.
7. Robert F. Kennedy, page 39.
8. Robert Dalleck, page 536.
9. Michael Lynch, page 128.
10. Robert Holmes, *A Spy Like No Other*, page 175.
11. CIA, 'President's Intelligence Checklist', 31 August 1962.
12. Michael Dobbs, page 46.

Chapter 4

1. Michael Lynch, page 126.
2. Michael Dobbs, pages 27 & 62.
3. Juanita Castro, *Life* magazine, August 1964.
4. David Talbot, *Brothers*, Simon & Schuster, London, 2007, page 163.
5. Quoted in 'Foreword', Arthur Schlesinger, page 12.
6. Quoted in Robert Dalleck, page 541.

Chapter 5

1. www.thisdayinaviation.com/richard-s-heyser
2. www.defencemedianetwork.com/stories/U-2-pilot-maj-rudy-anderson
3. Wikipedia, ibid.
4. Robert F. Kennedy, page 20.
5. David Talbot, page 164.
6. www.nsarchive.org National Security Archive – 'The Pentagon during the Cuban Missile Crisis'.
7. Robert F. Kennedy, page 29.
8. John F. Kennedy, quoted in Wikipedia, ibid.
9. *The Florida Times-Union*, Jacksonville, 20 October 2012.
10. Ibid.
11. Richard E. Neustadt & Graham T. Allison, page 112.

Chapter 6

1. Robert F. Kennedy, pages 38–39.
2. USNI News (US Naval Institute), 24 October 2010.
3. Wikipedia, ibid.
4. Report of seminar, 'RAF Bomber Command and the Cuban Missile Crisis, Oct 1962', London, 2012.
5. Ibid.
6. John F. Kennedy, Address to the American People, October 1962.
7. Ibid.
8. Ibid.
9. Interview with Ray Dalton, October 2016.
10. John F. Kennedy, ibid.
11. Quoted in Michael Dobbs, pages 53–54.
12. Fidel Castro's speech to the Cuban people, quoted in Michael Dobbs, page 74.
13. Quoted in Robert F. Kennedy, page 62.
14. *The Florida Times-Union*, Jacksonville, 24 October 1962.

Chapter 7

1. Robert F. Kennedy, page 52.
2. *The Florida Times-Union*, Jacksonville, 23 October 1962.

3. *Daily Sketch*, 23 October 23 1962, page 1.
4. *The Observer*, 28 October 1963, page 2.
5. Richard Dimbleby, quoted on P prune website.
6. *Western Mail*, 23 October 1962, page 1.
7. Robert Holmes, page 199.
8. Robert F. Kennedy, page 66.
9. Nikita Khrushchev, Letter to President Kennedy, 26 October 1963.
10. John F. Kennedy, Letter to Premier Khrushchev, 26 October 1963.
11. Nikita Khrushchev, ibid.

Chapter 8

1. Robert F. Kennedy, page 71.
2. www.defencemedianetwork.com
3. www.spartacus-international Cuban Missile Crisis
4. The Kennedy Tapes, now released into public domain.
5. John F. Kennedy, 26 October, ibid.
6. Robert F. Kennedy, page 80.
7. Michael Dobbs, pages 101–102.

Chapter 9

1. Sue Reid, 'The Day Britain Was 15 Minutes from Triggering Armageddon', in *Mail on Sunday*, 25 September 2008.
2. www.ploughshares.org
3. Sue Reid, ibid.
4. USNI News, ibid.
5. *Peace News*, October 2012.
6. Robert Nisbet, *Merlin's Lane: 24 Poems*, Prolebooks, 2011, and *The Interpreter's House* magazine, No. 47.
7. *Western Mail*, 24 October 1962.
8. Wikipedia, ibid.

Chapter 10

1. Wikipedia, ibid.
2. CIA, 'President's Intelligence Checklist', 28 October 1964.
3. Nikita Khrushchev, Letter to President Kennedy, 28 October 1962.
4. John Smith, 'The Cuban Missile Crisis', in *History Today*, March 2007.
5. Robert Kennedy, page 84.
6. CIA National Photographic Interpretation Centre, 'Report on Soviet Missile Sites on Cuba', undated.
7. John F. Kennedy, Address to the Nation, 2 November 1962.
8. *Western Mail*, 28 October 1962.
9. CIA, 'State of Soviet Military Personnel in Cuba', 30 December 1963.
10. Wikipedia, ibid.

Chapter 11

1. Winston Churchill, quoted in *New York Times*, 27 January 1954, page 1.
2. Quoted in Michael Lynch, page 127.
3. Robert McNamara, 'Forty Years After 13 Days', in *Arms Control America.*
4. www.armscontrol.org
5. Lynch, page 129.
6. Obituary, 'Richard Stephen Heyser', in *Los Angeles Times*, 13 October 2008.

Chapter 12

1. *Western Mail*, 26 October 1962.
2. Andrew Marr, 'The Invention of Marxism's Mr Cool' in *Sunday Times*, 27 November 2016.
3. Wikipedia, ibid.
4. John le Carré, *The Pigeon Tunnel*, Viking, London, 2016.

BIBLIOGRAPHY

Books

Dalleck, Robert, *John F. Kennedy: An Unfinished Life*. (Allen Lane, London, 2003)

Dobbs, Michael, *One Minute to Midnight*. (Arrow, London, 2008)

Hanhimaki, Jussi & Westad, Odd Arne, *The Cold War*. (OUP, London, 2004)

Holmes, Robert, *A Spy Like No Other*. (Biteback Press, London, 2012)

Kennedy, Robert F., *Thirteen Days*. (W.W. Norton & Co, London and New York, 1971)

le Carré, John, *The Pigeon Tunnel*. (Viking, London, 2016)

Lynch, Michael, *Stalin and Khrushchev: The USSR 1924–1964*. (Hodder & Stoughton, London, 2001)

McCall Smith, Alexander, *Emma*. (The Borough Press, London, 2015)

Nisbet, Robert, *Merlin's Lane: 24 Poems*. (Prolebooks, North Wales, 2011)

Sandbrook, Dominic, *White Heat*. (Little Brown, London, 2006)

Seldon, Esther, *The Life and Times of Fidel Castro*. (Parragon, London, 1994)

Talbot, David, *Brothers*. (Simon & Schuster, London, 2007)

Thomson, David, *England in the Twentieth Century*, (Penguin, London, 1965)

Articles/Reports

Castro, Juanita, 'My Brother is a Tyrant', *Life* magazine, Vol 57, No. 9, August 1964.

CIA Reports/Documents – www.cia.gov/library/readingroom/search/site/cuba

Neustadt, Richard E., & Allison, Graham T., 'Afterword', *Thirteen Days*.

Schlesinger, Arthur, 'Foreword', *Thirteen Days*.

Reid, Sue, 'The Day Britain was 15 Minutes from Triggering Armageddon', in *Mail on Sunday*, 26 September 2008.

Krushchev, Sergei & Lagronne, Sam, interview, USNI News.

Smith, John, 'The Cuban Missile Crisis', in *History Today*, March 2007.

Theses/Unpublished Works

Holmes, Ann-Marie, 'The United States and Cuba, 1898–1959', MA in Diplomacy and Military Studies, October 2009.

Anon., Report and minutes of seminar, 'RAF Bomber Command and the Cuban Missile Crisis', London, 2012.

Speeches (available online)

John F. Kennedy, 22 October & 2 November 1962.

Nikita Khrushchev, 28 October 1962.

Magazines and Newspapers

BBC News Magazine, 13 October 2012.
Daily Sketch, 23 October 1962.
The Florida Times-Union, 22–28 October 1962, 20 & 21 October 2012.
History Today, March 2007.
Life magazine, Vol. 57, No. 9, August 1964.
Los Angeles Times, 13 October 2008.
New York Times, 27 January 1954
The Observer, Sunday, 28 October 1962.
Peace News, October 2012.
Sunday Times, 27 November 2016.
USNI News, 24 October 2010.
Western Mail, October–November 1963.

Web Sites/Other Sources

www.armscontrol.org Article by Robert McNamara.
www.defencemedianetwork.com stories/U-2-pilot-maj-rudy-anderson.
www.nsarchive.org the Pentagon during the Cuban Missile Crisis.
www.thisdayinaviation.com Richard-S-Heyser.
www.ploughshares.org Cuban Missile Crisis.
www.wikipedia.org Cuban Missile Crisis.
www.spartacus-international Cuban Missile Crisis.
www.ppruneforums.org

Recordings/DVDs

John F Kennedy: A Memorial Album, long-playing record, No. 1000A, Diplomat Records, New Jersey.
The Kennedy Tapes, recordings of all EXCOMM meetings.
Vulcans, Victors and Cuba, DVD by Simply Media.

Interviews

Interviews with people remembering the crisis (see text, principally Chapter 9), all held by the author. Some were first published in *The Florida Times-Union*.

ACKNOWLEDGEMENTS

Grateful thanks to the following:

All those who so willingly gave me their views on, and memories of, the Cuban Missile Crisis of 1962.

The British V-bomber crews who happily told me of their hopes, fears and tasks during those few terrifying weeks.

Squadron Leader Ken Deveson, rugby-playing comrade from school days, himself a V-bomber pilot, for his expertise and contacts.

Roger MacCallum, yet another rugby-playing friend, for his technical knowledge and skill. As ever, Rog, you're a star.

Bob and Anne Howells, late of Pembroke Dock, now living in Jacksonville, Florida, for their unfailing hospitality and willingness to 'ferry me around'.

Robert Nisbet for allowing me to quote in full his poem.

ABOUT THE AUTHOR

Phil Carradice is a poet, novelist and historian. He has written over fifty books, the most recent being *The Call-up: A Study of Peacetime Conscription in Britain* and *Napoleon in Defeat and Captivity*. He presents the BBC Wales history programme *The Past Master* and is a regular broadcaster on both TV and radio. A native of Pembroke Dock, he now lives in the Vale of Glamorgan but travels extensively in the course of his work. Educated at Cardiff University and at Cardiff College of Education, Phil Carradice is a former head teacher but now lives as a full-time writer and is regarded as one of Wales's best creative writing tutors.